A G 7 J

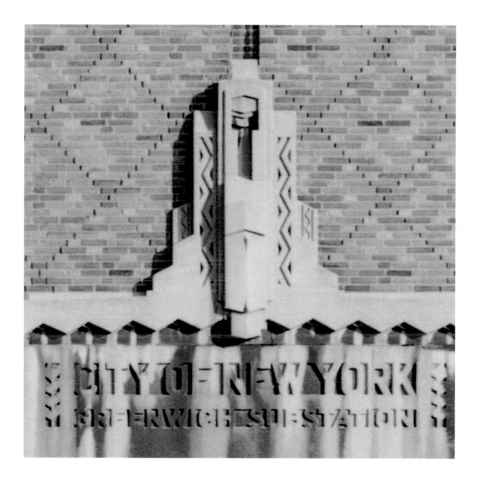

SUBWAY STYLE

100 YEARS OF ARCHITECTURE & DESIGN IN THE NEW YORK CITY SUBWAY

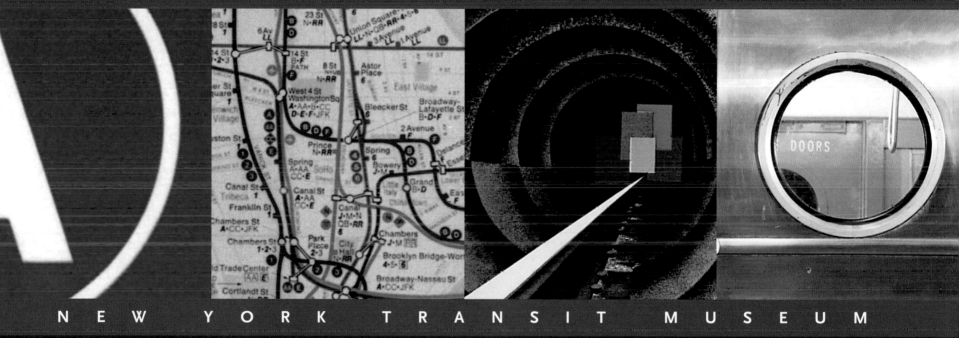

NEW YORK TRANSIT MUSEUM

Introduction by **JOSEPH GIOVANNINI** *Original photography by* **ANDREW GARN**

STEWART, TABORI & CHANG | NEW YORK

i: Detail, IND Greenwich Avenue Substation, 1932; **vi-vii:** Station
Entrance at Municipal Building, Chambers Street IRT Station;
ix: Wall Street IRT Station Plaque, 1905; **237:** 50th Street IRT Station
Faience Plaque, "50", 1904; **242:** Model, R-142 Subway Train, 1999.
Photographs copyright © by Andrew Garn. | **iv-v:** Car 3004,
Circa 1935; **233:** Car 2424, Circa 1920 **235:** Drawing, Standard Kiosk.
Courtesy of the New York Transit Museum.

Published in 2004 by
Stewart, Tabori & Chang, 115 West 18th Street, New York, NY 10011

Canadian Distribution:
Canadian Manda Group, One Atlantic Avenue, Suite 105
Toronto, Ontario M6K 3E7, Canada

Library of Congress Cataloging-in-Publication Data
New York Transit Museum.
   Subway style : 100 years of architecture & design in
the New York City subway / introduction by Joseph Giovannini ;
original photography by Andrew Garn.
       p. cm.
   Includes bibliographical references and index.
   ISBN 1-58479-349-X
1. Subway station—New York (State)—New York—Design and
construction—Exhibitions. I. Title.
TF847.N5G37 2004
725'.31'09747107—dc22   2004004255

Printed in China

10 9 8 7 6 5 4 3 2 1

FIRST PRINTING

Stewart, Tabori & Chang is a subsidiary of

LA MARTINIÈRE
GROUPE

Contents

INTRODUCTION

There are two mental maps of New York City, one above ground, and the other below, the first showing the city as separation, and the second, as connection. The conventional map documents boroughs divided by bodies of water; the underground map shows subways stitching the boroughs together, making the city one.

In New York, subways are geography: their tracery underground defines the extent of a city that the lines themselves transformed and even spawned. Before the underground map, the land map was the principal cartographic truth, but with the subway's advent and tentacular spread, the subterranean map emerged as the operative route for the city's commuting millions.

Today, on its centennial, New Yorkers think of this underground realm as a single system. But before their unification in 1940, there were the IRT, BMT, and IND lines, and each rival company built a separate network with its own engineers, architects, and designers. Often even subway stops within each line differed from each other, by design. From the start, visual distinction typified the overall system, and the diversity deepened across time as successive designers operated on their respective systems implementing incremental change. When New York City eventually took control of all three systems, merging them, a certain visual system-

atization took place, such as the design of the metal-and-glass token booths, and more recently, the card dispensers and turnstiles. But still, a critical mass of designed artifacts was already cemented in place, and the system overall remains one of difference rather than similarity: heterogeneity prevails. It would hardly be possible to compile this book on Paris's subway system because of the Napoleonic uniformity of France's top-down, governmentally initiated, bureaucratically-controlled project.

In a poetically impressionistic rather than encyclopedic way, this volume documents the cumulative differences across systems, time, designers, and styles, from the initial City Beautiful movement through Arts and Crafts, Machine Age design, Art Deco, Moderne, and the Bauhaus. Each new decade brought its own design sensibility, layering design strata in an underground that evolved into a visual palimpsest. With adaptations, upgrades and reconfigurations, the subways became an unself-conscious design repository of design thinking over the decades, and today, as the following pages show, the underground constitutes a "found" museum. Benches alone have their own history, not to mention the typographic fonts still scripted into ceramic signs, plus metal grills secreted in unobserved places. Over the last several decades, the arts program, featuring site-specific

viii | SUBWAY STYLE

installations that are never repeated, has compounded what can only be called the subway's systematic uniqueness.

In a city symbolized by towers that aspire to the sky, it is the subway network that makes the commutes possible, and the city work. New York's famous skyscrapers are the foreground to the subway's background, the solid to the void, the seen to the unseen. *Subway Style: 100 Years of Architecture and Design in the New York City Subway* inverts the usual image of New York, making the invisible visible, bringing the underground to light, collecting an unexpected quarry of visual history. The book captures one hundred years of design in this amazingly complex, largely uncelebrated environment.

On a personal note: I would like to pay witness to the edifying role that subway design plays in the everyday life of the city. The graphic designers of the subway system have built into the system an exercise in progressive education. The visual punch of all those letters and numbers on the 1, 2, 3, 4, 5, 6 and 7 lines, and the A, B, E, F, R, M, N, Q and W routes, each bulleted in a colorful circle, attracted the attention of my toddling Manhattan-born daughter, and taught her numbers and letters long before she ever would have learned them in the above-ground world.

STATIONS AND STRUCTURES

Modern New York is inconceivable without its subway system, that vast maze of underground tunnels and overhead trestles—656 miles of track connecting 468 stations—serving millions of people every day. To straphangers, the subway can seem like a strictly utilitarian environment of steel and concrete, bright lights and screeching wheels.

Yet from the beginning, the people who planned the subway's construction considered it, in words actually written into the contract, a "great public work," worthy of attractive design, even of "beauty." Neglect on the one hand and renovation on the other have taken their toll, but the subway is still a place of art and architecture, from the stations and the

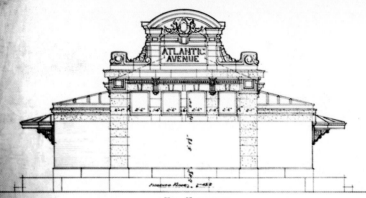
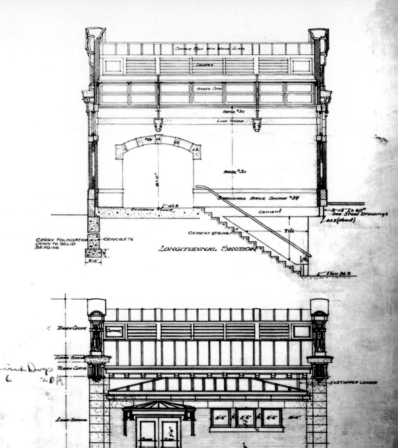
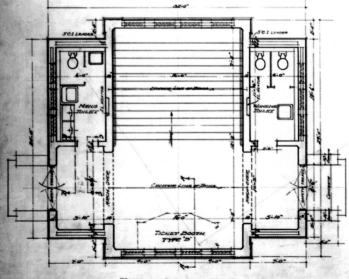

powerhouses and the rolling stock, to the furniture, signs, maps, and even the advertisements.

Conceived in the 1890s, the subway owes its existence to visionaries of the Victorian era, the same age that produced such great public works as Central Park, the Croton water system, and the Brooklyn Bridge, and culminated, in 1898, in the consolidation of the five boroughs into the City of Greater New York. Street trolleys and elevated trains offered service along many routes, but the far more comprehensive subway quickly grew into the linchpin of a transportation system tying the boroughs together—not for nothing was the original service called "Interborough Rapid Transit" (IRT)—and in so doing made possible the modern metropolis we know today.

Design and aesthetics have been part of the subway from the original stations of 1904 to the latest work in 2004. But nothing in New York stands still—certainly not the subway—and the approach to subway style has evolved, reflecting the major stages of the system's construction during the early 1900s, the teens, and the late '20s and early '30s and the renovations and redesigns of later years. The earliest parts of the system still convey the flowery, genteel flavor of a smaller, older city. Later sections, by contrast, show a conscious turn toward the modern, including open admiration for the system's raw structural power. The evolution of subway design follows the trajectory of the world of art and architecture as these came to terms with the Industrial Revolution, and the tug-of-war between a traditional deference to European models and a modernist ideology demanding an honest expression of contemporary industrial technology.

DRAWING, ATLANTIC AVENUE CONTROL HOUSE
1906
Brooklyn
Heins & LaFarge, architects

116TH STREET IRT CONTROL HOUSE
1904
Manhattan
Heins & LaFarge, architects
Though just as fanciful as the 72nd Street control house, the more compact version that once stood at West 116th Street in Manhattan had to fit onto a smaller traffic island.

WINDSCREEN
Fort Hamilton Parkway BMT Station, Brooklyn
Station opened 1916; photograph taken March 24, 1964
At Fort Hamilton Parkway—as at most Dual Contracts stations—a frieze of ceramic tile brings color and geometry to the platform walls. More ceramics can be found in the overhang of the concrete windscreen: Guastavino tiles set in a herringbone pattern. The tiles take their name from the father-and-son team of immigrant Catalan architects (both named Rafael) who imported and perfected the technique of thin-tile-and-cement vaulting.

207TH STREET STATION
June 22, 1906, Manhattan
What's an elevated subway doing in such a rustic area? Thanks to the new IRT service, the countryside surrounding the 207th Street station didn't stay rustic for long; it quickly developed into the crowded urban neighborhood of Inwood. The station itself—like those serving the city's nineteenth-century elevated trains—has the look of a Swiss chalet.

The first part of the subway to open—the original IRT of 1904—consisted of a single line running from City Hall Park up the east side of Manhattan to Grand Central, west across 42nd Street to Times Square, and north up the West Side into what was still the Bronx countryside. Opening day brought crowds of New Yorkers to see their city's latest public work, a major piece of urban design exemplifying the newly fashionable City Beautiful movement. The subway's chief engineer, William Barclay Parsons, had supervised the system's construction, but he had also brought in outside architectural talent: Heins & LaFarge, designers of the Cathedral of St. John the Divine and the Bronx Zoo, and the legendary Stanford White, master of European-style classicism.

Parsons had long experience in the transit field and had traveled to Europe to visit the handful of cities—including London, Paris, and Budapest—that already had functioning subways. He aimed to build a system combining "efficiency" and "beauty," as demanded by the construction contract. Efficiency would have come naturally to an engineer, but Parsons also worked in a climate dominated by an urban reform movement that aimed to reshape American civic centers with grand, classically-inspired marble palaces laid out along broad boulevards in symmetrical plans. The City Beautiful especially favored the overscaled columns and arches and sculptural ornament imported from Paris by American graduates of the École des Beaux-Arts (School of Fine Arts). The opening of the subway in 1904 prompted a *New York Sun* headline celebrating "The City Beautiful: Its Beginnings Underground."

Heins & LaFarge brought with them a beaux arts sensibility, but also a distaste for what LaFarge called "servile, thoughtless imitation, the making of dull, lifeless, archaeological copies of the works of long dead hands." Given the opportunity to design an entire station—the City Hall station, originally planned as the subway's grand entrance—they produced a remarkable brick-and-tile space whose ceiling of Guastavino vaults, faced in broad, white terra-cotta tiles set off by green and brown tiles at the edges, arched over the loop formed by the tracks. One magazine hailed the station as "an apotheosis of curves." Chandeliers, oak furnishings, and decorative faience plaques inscribed "City Hall" certainly added to the effect, but the station owed its design to its shape and materials.

In the remaining stations, on the other hand, Heins & LaFarge found their role limited to designing a decorative overlay for the steel and concrete boxes planned by engineers. Faced with uninterrupted walls the length of five train cars, rows of unadorned steel girders along the platform edge, and ceilings of concrete vaults, the architects re-imagined the stations as distant cousins of turn-of-the-century drawing rooms. They dressed up the steel girders as round columns; used classical ornament, glass tiles, and mosaics to divide the walls into panels matching the spaces between the columns; and hid the vaults with flat suspended plaster ceilings divided into panels by classical moldings. And they ensured that each station differed in ornament and color scheme from its neighbors on the route.

At street level, Heins & LaFarge got to design handsome ornamental cast-iron kiosks to shelter entrances and exits, as well as

STATION ENTRANCE AT MUNICIPAL BUILDING
Chambers Street IRT Station
Station opened 1918
Manhattan

POSTCARD
"City Hall Subway Station, New York"
1904
Heins & LaFarge, architects
The graceful, rhythmic patterns of the medieval-inspired vaulting and arches that support the massive structure of City Hall station—along with its concave leaded-glass skylights and elaborate electric chandeliers— make this station the beaux arts jewel of the subway system.

BAY PARKWAY BMT STATION
January 6, 1917
Brooklyn
Squire J. Vickers, architect
To avoid the enormous expense of underground construction, many of the Dual Contracts lines outside Manhattan were built as elevated structures. Unlike the earlier IRT chalet-style elevated stations, however, Vickers's work looks distinctly industrial. Steel-and-concrete stations like this one on Bay Parkway rely on the repetition of heavy rectangular forms to create an effect of massiveness, slightly softened by bands of ornamental tile.

QUEENS BOULEVARD VIADUCT
Opened 1917
Queens
This mile-long viaduct required 20,000 square feet of ornamental colored tile—necessitating the largest tile contract of its day.

a handful of brick-and-stone entrance pavilions (called "control houses") and half a dozen power substations, but they lost out on by far the grandest of the subway's aboveground structures, the enormous, main powerhouse at 58th and 59th streets between 11th and 12th avenues. There, the transit company's directors found themselves caught between the modernist instinct for structural expression and the beaux arts requirements of the City Beautiful. In the end, instead of approving "a powerhouse of massive and simple design," the directors accepted an offer from Stanford White to design a "French Renaissance" powerhouse with classical pilasters framing huge window arches and classical ornamental details in terra-cotta. Grand as it was, White's work amounted to an enormous shell, a freestanding structure surrounding, and essentially disguising, two separate industrial buildings. Only the tall chimneys rising into the skyline suggested what might lie behind the palace walls.

The second major phase of construction—in the years just before and after World War I—involved both the IRT and the BRT (Brooklyn Rapid Transit, later the BMT, or Brooklyn-Manhattan Transit), a company with long experience operating Brooklyn's trolleys and elevated lines. Together, the IRT and BRT—in what became known as the Dual Contracts—extended the subway's reach deep into the Bronx, Brooklyn, and Queens. With Heins & LaFarge's contract long since ended, the design work was brought in-house and turned over to Squire J. Vickers, a young architect and accomplished painter who had joined the subway staff in 1906 and would stay for thirty-six years. The Dual Contracts more than

59TH STREET POWERHOUSE
Opened 1904
Manhattan
Stanford White of McKim, Mead & White, architect
Occupying an entire city block, this enormous plant powered the entire IRT subway
and was the single largest user of electricity in its day. Though clearly marked as an
industrial structure by its enormous chimneys, the powerhouse is effectively hidden
behind the grand classical colonnades of Stanford White's "French Renaissance"
façades, indicative of the City Beautiful movement of the time.

WEEP HOLE GRILLE
Wall Street IRT Station
1905
Manhattan
Even such small construction details as weep holes—which let
moisture escape from subway station walls—inspired elegantly
designed metalwork from Heins & LaFarge.

doubled the size of the original system. Heins & LaFarge may have been better-known architects, but Vickers determined the aesthetics of most of the subway system.

Vickers learned the beaux arts approach to architecture at Cornell University, but by the time he got to the subway, he had moved in the direction of the English Arts and Crafts movement. If City Beautiful advocates hoped to mask the grim necessities of industrial life with an illusion of formal classicism, the founders of the Arts and Crafts movement hoped instead to fight back: to champion the personal work of the craftsman over the anonymous work of the factory and to recognize the virtue of simplicity over grandeur, of usefulness over symbolism. Arts and Crafts found its way into the subway as early as 1904, in the so-called Craftsman-style wooden benches of the original IRT. But it was Vickers who brought the movement to the subway in a big way, especially with his ceramics and metalwork.

Faced with the same steel-and-concrete box stations that Heins & LaFarge had tried to disguise, Vickers chose to celebrate the subway's underlying industrial character, exposing concrete vault ceilings and leaving steel girders unadorned. "Bearing in mind the utilitarian nature of the subway," he wrote, "this severity of design seems to us the most appropriate treatment." At the same time, following his Arts and Crafts instincts, Vickers hoped to alleviate some of that severity with brightly colored geometric tiles: "It is not enough that our stations should be sanitary, commodious and convenient—they must at the same time present a cheerful and attractive appearance to the public." Colored tiles on the walls should "blaze with the brightness of a jewel," providing a "joyous note like a banner flung from the frowning window of a castle." Aboveground, Vickers designed the elevated line along Queens Boulevard as an enormous structure of reinforced concrete but added "a continuous band of colored tile with a plaque on each column . . . to give the gray surface a touch of color."

Up to this point, the city had financed the system's construction but leased it out to the private sector to equip and operate. In the third stage of construction, between 1925 and 1940, the city not only built a new line, but also undertook to run it independently of the existing private operators—hence the name "Independent." The IND ran under Sixth and Eighth Avenues in Manhattan, the Grand Concourse in the Bronx, Fulton Street in Brooklyn, and Queens Boulevard. Squire Vickers, still hard at work for the subway, designed the new stations, but almost a generation had passed since the days of his Arts and Crafts approach. Vickers' work now reflected the aesthetics of the Machine Age—a frank embrace of modern industry, with its new forms and materials, expressed in the zigzag geometry of Art Deco or the streamlined curves of the Moderne.

Belowground, the new line offered larger and more spacious stations, but economic considerations limited ornament to long strips of colored tile along the wall. Aboveground, however, Vickers found greater opportunity. At the elevated station bridging Fourth Avenue at Ninth Street in Brooklyn, he created a typically

DETAIL, STONE FLOWER
Wall Street IRT Station
1904
Manhattan

Machine Age design: four steel supporting arches framed by two large towers in patterned brick, which he described as "simple with but little detail and few openings in order that the mass may give the desired buttress effect." Vickers also designed two power substations in Manhattan, one at 53rd Street and another on Greenwich Street, using "light gray tapestry brick with variations in shade" and an aluminum door with "a satin finish" and a design "etched with acid."

In 1940, New York City united and took control of all three systems, a consolidation described as the largest railroad merger in American history. In the following decades, few new stations joined the subway. Two reorganizations—creating the New York City Transit Authority in 1953 and then the Metropolitan Transportation Authority in 1968—involved attempts at expansion, including the 63rd Street Tunnel and the Archer Avenue/Jamaica Center line, both opened in the late 1980s. In keeping with the post–World War II, International Style thinking that took to heart such slogans as "less is more" and "ornament is crime," the 1950s, '60s, and '70s saw station renovations reflecting the belief that the subway's historic design had become hopelessly outdated and that progress and technological advances demanded the removal of old-fashioned decorative detail. The architectural firm of Johnson/Burgee redesigned the 49th Street (BMT Broadway local) station with prefabricated units, glazed orange structural brick, and cantilevered stone benches, intending it to be the prototype for a "New Stations Program" that was ultimately abandoned.

In the meantime, the subway entered a period of decline—reduced service and increased crime.

In the subway's most recent transformation, begun in the 1980s, huge infusions of capital have brought the system back from the brink of collapse. At the same time, as part of the growing national interest in historic preservation, the original subway designs have been rediscovered and now command a new respect. In 1991, New York City Transit retained the architectural firm of Prentice, Chan & Olhausen to establish station renovation guidelines. New station makeovers now combine historic restoration with smart contemporary design. And today's New Yorkers can look back on one hundred years of surprisingly captivating art and architecture in a place where most probably never thought to look for it—the subway.

49TH STREET BMT STATION
Renovated 1973
Manhattan
Philip Johnson and John Burgee, architects
Reflecting the idealism of the recently established MTA, this station was created as a prototype for a "New Stations Program" by internationally renowned architects Philip Johnson and John Burgee. Johnson described the station design of vermillion glazed brick, white terrazzo floors, and indirect fluorescent lighting in a *New York Times* article: "Cheer is the word, like a big shopping center." This renovation is most notable for its pioneering use of sound-muffling materials installed in the tunnel ceiling and at track level.

IND GREENWICH AVENUE SUBSTATION
1932
Manhattan
Squire J. Vickers, architect
Chief architect Vickers's façade design of
warm gray tapestry-brick-and-limestone
trim reflects his desire to make substations
blend into the residential districts that
surrounded them.

DETAILS, SUBSTATION 41
Opened in 1917
Manhattan, West 16th Street
The Arts and Crafts brickwork on the
exterior of this substation stands in sharp
contrast to the industrial machines
contained inside to power numerous
subway lines, signals, and station lighting.

IRT SUBSTATION 17
Opened 1906
Manhattan, Dyckman Street
The distinctive wrought-iron
roof brackets on this substation
recall the pioneering work of
architect Ernest Flagg.

NINTH AVENUE BMT STATION CONTROL HOUSE
November 23, 1915
Brooklyn

NINTH AVENUE BMT STATION
Station opened 1915
Brooklyn
Though designed by in-house architects, the horizontal composition, casement windows, brick and terra-cotta work, and hipped roof of this control house has something of the flavor of the work of Frank Lloyd Wright and the Prairie School.

CLOSED TRACKS
Ninth Avenue BMT Station
Station opened 1915
Brooklyn
This photo illustrates the basic structural system of the subway lines built between 1904 and 1928. The slender steel columns, bracketed beams, and tunnel arches inspired Vickers's station ornament.

RENDERING
Proposal for Board of Transportation Building,
370 Jay Street, Brooklyn
Circa 1935
Eggers & Higgins, architects
The architectural firm of Eggers & Higgins
proposed this dignified, if modest, Art Deco
office building prior to World War II.

WATERCOLOR RENDERING
Proposal for Board of Transportation Building,
370 Jay Street, Brooklyn
Circa 1935
Squire J. Vickers, architect
Courtesy of MTA New York City Transit,
Capital Program Management

FRONT ELEVATION

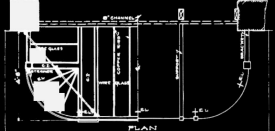

PLAN

DRAWING
IRT Station Control House
1908
Heins & LaFarge, architects
Heins & LaFarge designed six fanciful
Flemish Renaissance-inspired brick-and-stone
IRT control houses of which three survive:
Bowling Green and West 72nd Street in
Manhattan and Atlantic Avenue in Brooklyn.
Three others, at West 103rd, West 116th,
and West 149th streets in Manhattan,
disappeared long ago. This drawing is almost
identical in detail to the central portion
of the 72nd Street version, except for a
handsome cast-iron marquee projecting
out over the entrance.

72ND STREET IRT CONTROL HOUSE
Station opened 1904; restored 2003
Manhattan

72ND STREET CONTROL HOUSE NORTH
Opened 2002
Manhattan
*Gruzen Samton and Richard Dattner &
Partners, architects*
Architects Gruzen Samton and Richard
Dattner & Partners solved the chronic
overcrowding in the 72nd Street Control
House by designing this new structure across
the street—a contemporary re-imagining
of Heins & LaFarge's original. Natural light
now streams into the restored station below,
while at street level a newsstand / coffee-
bar kiosk and plaza seating contribute to the
vitality of local street-life.

STATION ENTRANCE
Bowling Green IRT Station
Circa 1960; demolished 1971
Manhattan
For just over a decade, the Bowling Green station had a classic International
Style, steel-and-glass entrance on the north to offset its original Flemish
Renaissance–inspired, brick-and-stone entrance on the south.

STATION MODERNIZATION RENDERING
Bowling Green IRT Station
Circa 1970
Manhattan
New York City Transit, architects

BOWLING GREEN
STATION
MODERNIZATION
DESIGNED BY
...TA ARCHITECTS

ROCKAWAY VIADUCT

Built 1939–1942; operated by New York City Transit after 1956

Queens

Created by Robert Moses for the Long Island Rail Road, this reinforced concrete viaduct was constructed as part of his larger park plan for the Rockaway Peninsula. It was designed to permit the operation of subway trains if the railroad line was taken over by the city. This became a reality in 1956 as New York City Transit Authority trains rolled across Jamaica Bay, connecting Rockaway with the rest of the city.

DETAIL, BRICKWORK

Fourth Avenue IND Station

1933

Brooklyn

DETAIL, ARCH

Fourth Avenue IND Station

1933

Brooklyn

According to Squire J. Vickers, the announcement of plans for an elevated station at Fourth Avenue caused an angry reaction from local residents. "But," he wrote, "they were persuaded that the structure would adorn rather than desecrate the avenue; then we were directed to make an architectural gesture." The photo shows a structural steel arch with infill of glass and cast-aluminum Art Deco zigzags.

DETAIL, METALWORK
Manhattan Valley Viaduct Arch, 125th Street IRT Station
Circa 1903
Manhattan
Due to the dramatic ups and downs of upper Manhattan's geography, the IRT subway—most of its stations generally just a flight of stairs below street level—bursts into the open between West 116th and 135th streets. The 2,174-foot-long steel viaduct carrying the tracks rises high above 125th Street, supported by an enormous, double-hinged parabolic braced arch spanning 168½ feet.

ROCKAWAY VIADUCT
Built 1939–1942
Queens

PORTAL OF FORT GEORGE TUNNEL
Opened 1906
Manhattan
The Fort George Tunnel—the longest subway tunnel bored through solid rock—commemorated those who lost their lives during its perilous construction with a beaux arts inspired portal.

ENTRANCE AND PASSAGEWAY
53rd Street / Fifth Avenue IRT Station
Opened 1989
Manhattan
In return for extra height and more rentable
floor space, the developer of an adjacent
skyscraper helped pay for this new passenger
connection between the Lexington IRT and
53rd Street IND lines. Belowground, natural
daylight illuminates a brightly colored,
spacious concourse, while at the street-level
entrance, a striking wedge of glass invites
passengers into the system.

180TH STREET IND STATION
Station opened 1932
Manhattan
Part of a unique design—responding to the
station's location deep beneath the bluff of
Washington Heights—this mezzanine is
suspended from the tunnel roof by vertical steel
supports, resulting in column-free platforms.
Extended horizontally, the steel supports also serve
as lighting standards for the platforms below.

21ST STREET / QUEENSBRIDGE IND STATION
Station designed 1969; opened 1989
Queens
Emblematic of the optimism of the MTA's 1969 plan for new lines is the handsome
architectural finish and spaciousness of this station. Because it took twenty years for
the station to be built, a significant design lag is evident in the final product.

PROSPECT PARK BMT STATION
Station opened 1920; renovated 1994/2002
Brooklyn
The Americans with Disabilities Act (ADA) mandates that substantial renovations of public transit facilities eliminate barriers to accessibility. New York City Transit station renovation guidelines, on the other hand, mandate respect for historic design elements. The design for an elevator and open-air mezzanine at this station incorporates both.

FACETED GLASS WINDSCREENS
Franklin Avenue Shuttle BMT Station
1999
Brooklyn
MTA Arts for Transit; Eric Pryor, artist
Stained glass is not used often on elevated subway stations, but it was a common decorative element in the stations of New York City's nineteenth-century elevated lines.

161ST STREET / YANKEE STADIUM IND STATION
Station opened 1917
Bronx
Thanks to current design guidelines, the recent renovation of the 161st Street station preserved the original light standards and refurbished the metal roof canopy. It also called for a new windscreen of fireproof aluminum and impact-resistant glass—replacing the solid corrugated wall from the mid-1960s that had, in turn, replaced the original wood-and-glass version—so that baseball fans can once again enjoy views of Yankee Stadium.

MODEL, IND STATION
Roosevelt Avenue / 74th Street Station
Circa 2000
Model-maker unknown
Project Designed by MTA New York City Transit and
Fox & Fowle Architects
Courtesy of MTA New York Ciy Transit, Capital
Program Management

MODEL, COMPLEX REHABILITATION
BMT Myrtle Avenue / Wyckoff Avenue Station
September 2003; project completion scheduled for 2007
Brooklyn
Model by Todd Architectural Models, Somerville, New Jersey
Station rehabilitation designed by Richard Dattner &
Partners, architects, with Parsons-Brinckerhoff, engineers
Courtesy of MTA New York City Transit, Capital
Program Management
The model for the extensive rehabilitation of a major
subway junction—between the elevated Wyckoff Avenue
station and the underground Myrtle Avenue station—
combines the preservation of historic features with
stylish contemporary design.

MODEL
Elevator Entrance at 125th Street IRT Station
Circa 1986; completed circa 1989
Model-maker unknown
Project designed by MTA New York City Transit
Courtesy of MTA New York City Transit, Capital Program Management
To provide ADA-compliant accessibility to the station at 125th Street and Lexington Avenue, an in-house team of architects and engineers developed this contemporary glass-and-metal design for a sidewalk kiosk entrance. The project was completed about 1989.

MODEL
Prototype Elevated Station Elevator, Stairs, and Windscreen with Canopy Roof
October 2002
Model by Saleh & Dirani Architectural Modeling, Inc., New York
Project designed by MTA New York City Transit
Courtesy of MTA New York City Transit, Capital Program Management
This model illustrates one approach to rehabilitating an elevated station—including the addition of an elevator to improve accessibility—while maintaining much of its original design. Although this particular model was never built, many similar examples have been constructed in the system.

MODEL

Proposed Second Avenue Subway Station

2003

Project designed by MTA New York City
Transit, DMJM+Harris, and
Fox & Fowle Architects

Proposals to build the Second Avenue
subway date back to 1929. In the early 1970s
construction began on several tunnel
segments but halted because of the city's
financial crisis at the end of the decade.
Construction to complete the project is
scheduled to begin at the end of 2004.

Delicately colored scenes of historic New York, bucolic images of beavers gnawing at trees, multicolored wreaths and horns of plenty, mosaics, faience, terra-cotta, glass tile—who could imagine such things surrounding the steel girders, concrete platforms, and endless corridors of the subways? Yet right from the start, the subway's planners hoped to soften

AIDING THE TRAVELER IN THE RAPID IDENTIFICATION OF HIS WHEREABOUTS

its hardest edges with the finest available ornamental design. And the most effective materials to use—bright and colorful, but also durable and inexpensive—were ceramics, made from baked ("fired") earth or clay.

William Barclay Parsons and Heins & LaFarge established the two-pronged philosophy that would govern subway ceramics for the next century. Parsons

33RD STREET IRT STATION MOSAIC
Station opened 1904
Manhattan
With the station name spelled out in ceramic tiles inside a rectangle with
a flowery beaux arts border, this panel exemplifies the ceramics of
Heins & LaFarge's first stations. The Fulton Street and Wall Street stations
have nearly identical panels.

FULTON STREET IRT STATION PLAQUE
Station opened 1905
Manhattan
Made by Rookwood Pottery, Cincinnati, Ohio
Robert Fulton—from whom lower Manhattan's Fulton Street takes its name—
didn't invent the steamboat, but he showed it could be profitable for this
commercial city surrounded by waterways. Heins & LaFarge's Rookwood
plaque imagines Fulton's *Clermont* steaming up the Hudson on a windy day.

had already determined that though the subway is utilitarian it
should also be beautiful; now Heins & LaFarge determined that
though ceramics are beautiful they should also be utilitarian. So
while the subway would be adorned with tiles fabricated by only the
finest firms—Rookwood Pottery, Grueby Faience, Atlantic Terra
Cotta—those ceramics would also serve, in LaFarge's words, "the distinct and proper purpose of aiding the traveler in the rapid and easy
identification of his whereabouts."

Heins & LaFarge took a variety of approaches to their task.
The simplest, most straightforward way to identify a station was to
write its name on the walls—using handsome ceramic tiles and
mosaics. A passenger on a train roaring into Times Square would see
the station's name spelled out in white letter tiles on a blue tile background, surrounded by a fanciful, curving, decorative border of
mosaic garlands and topped by the kind of beaux arts classical details
typical of the City Beautiful.

The second, more imaginative, approach identified not just
the station name but also its neighborhood. Some stations got symbols: a ceramic beaver for the fur-trading Astors of Astor Place, a
ceramic eagle grasping a shield with the number 33 for an armory at
the 33rd Street station. Others got historic scenes: Robert Fulton's
steamer paddling up the Hudson past green shores under a blue sky
at Fulton Street; a Dutch colonial house protected by the old wooden
stockade from which Wall Street takes its name at Wall Street; a
Spanish ship bringing Christopher Columbus to the New World at
Columbus Circle.

When Squire J. Vickers took over, he followed the existing model, focusing on the identification of stations and neighborhoods. But while Heins & LaFarge had favored elegant curves and elaborate, flowery designs, in ceramics projecting out from the walls, Vickers's work tended to the flat and rectangular, verging on the abstract. Part of this approach was practical: flat ceramics had no corners or crevices to collect dust. But more of it was philosophical, reflecting the influence of the Arts and Crafts movement.

Vickers spelled out station names in white tiles on a colored tile background but framed them in a simple rectangle, with a border of individual colored tiles—rectangular, square or diamond shaped—laid out flat against the wall. "The irregularity of these little pieces is quite necessary," he wrote, "for if this work is laid up in regular squares the charm is immediately lost." Vickers abandoned the use of neighborhood symbols, but he elaborated on city scenes, often taken from historic prints: a tavern on the long-vanished canal of Canal Street; Peter Stuyvesant's house ("Whitehall") for Whitehall Street; the Brooklyn Heights waterfront for Clark Street. Vickers designed some of these scenes himself; for others, he enlisted Jay Van Everen and Herbert Dole, painter friends from his university days. Vickers described the ceramic scenes as "plaques which nudge the memory to recall the past." But because those scenes are rendered in a broad-brush mosaic—individual pieces of colored tile fitted together to form an image—they have a distinctly abstract look, creating a modern image of the past.

For the IND, Vickers abandoned standard ornamentation altogether. He still relied on colored tile (violet, blue, green, yellow,

BOROUGH HALL IRT STATION MOSAIC
Station opened 1919, Brooklyn
Because construction of the Borough Hall station straddled World War I, its ornament includes both Heins & LaFarge's flowery beaux arts ceramics for the earlier Lexington line and Squire J. Vickers's flat and brightly colored Arts and Crafts mosaics. Vickers's tiles, hand-set in the factory, were brought to the station and applied section by section.

BOROUGH HALL IRT STATION PLAQUE
Station opened 1919, Brooklyn
Like so many of the scenes produced under Squire J. Vickers's supervision, this image of Borough Hall comes from a much older illustration. Here it's shown in its original role as Brooklyn's City Hall, before the five boroughs of New York were incorporated in 1898. Also included is the original steeple, destroyed by a fire in 1895.

CANAL STREET IND STATION
Manhattan
Thanks to new, preservation-minded guidelines, a major renovation of this station used advanced technology to re-create, rather than replace, its Machine Age IND bands of color tiles. While in 1932 the original four-inch-square tiles were laid by hand directly on the wall's concrete surface, the replacement tile was attached to a water-resistant fiberglass panel at the factory and then brought to the station. The panels were then bolted into place creating space for water seepage. The result: a tile wall, resistant to water damage, whose installation caused minimal service disruption.

WATERCOLOR DRAWING
"Color Chart of Stations on Independent Lines"
Circa 1930
Courtesy of MTA New York City Transit, Capital Program Management

red), but now the tiles formed flat bands running the length of each station and functioned as a color code: a wide color band at express stops, and narrower bands of an alternate color at the intervening local stops. Vickers explained: "For instance, 50th Street is violet, 59th Street is blue and the seven locals to the north are also blue. . . . In the stations below 42nd Street two shades of the same color are used. In stations north of 42nd Street the color is used with a black border. A person on a north-bound train who observes a blue band with a black border knows he is in the Central Park zone." Identification plaques in the stations combined white tiles with blocks of color. The abstract, geometric feeling of the IND suggested that subway design had finally surrendered to the Machine Age, an era in which the subway, with its endless parallel tracks and vertical steel girders, undoubtedly formed a component part.

During the following decades, no new decorative ceramics found their way into the subway. Today, however, under the direction of the MTA's Capital Program Management and Arts for Transit programs, when stations are renovated their ceramics are restored, not removed, and sometimes joined by new ones—mosaics of dancers and acrobats at Lincoln Center or the *Empress Voyage* at Canal Street. Subway ceramics have come full circle. And today, because of their history, those ceramics not only identify the system's stations and neighborhoods, but they can also—for the informed straphanger—identify the dates and designers of the stations and make it possible to read the history written on the subway walls.

COLOR CHART OF STATIONS ON INDEPENDENT LINES

RT. No 105 ÷ 207TH ST.	RT. 109 ÷ JAY ST.-BOROUGH HALL	RT. 103 * BROADWAY-LAFAYETTE ST.	RT. 108 * QUEENS PLAZA	RT. 110 LAFAYETTE AV.
DYCKMAN ST. 200TH ST	* BERGEN ST.	* SECOND AVE.	36TH ST.	CLINTON-WASHINGTON AV.
RT. No 78 ÷ 190TH ST.-OVERLOOK TERRACE	CARROLL ST.	DELANCEY ST.	STEINWAY ST.	FRANKLIN AV.
181ST ST.	SMITH-9TH ST. 4TH AVE. (EL. STNS. NO COLOR)	E. BROADWAY	46TH ST.	* NOSTRAND AV.
175TH ST.	* 7TH AVE.	YORK ST.	NORTHERN BLVD.	KINGSTON-THROOP AVE.
* 168TH ST.-BROAD'Y-MEDICAL CENT'R	15TH ST.-PROSPECT PARK		* 65TH ST.	* UTICA AVE.
163RD ST. AMSTRM AV.	FT. HAMILTON PARKWAY	RT. 106 155TH ST.-8TH AVE.	* ROOSEVELT AVE.	RALPH AV.
155TH ST.	* CHURCH AVE.	161ST ST.-RIVER AV.	ELMHURST AVE.	ROCKAWAY AV.
* 145TH ST.	RT. 107 ÷ COURT ST.	167TH ST.	GRAND AV.-NEWTOWN	* BROADWAY-EAST NEW YORK
135TH ST.	* HOYT-SCHERMERHORN ST.	170TH ST.	WOODHAVEN BLVD. SLATTERY PLAZA	LIBERTY AV.
* 125TH ST.	FULTON ST.	174TH-175TH STS.	63RD DRIVE	VAN SICLEN AV.
116TH ST.	CLINTON-WASHINGTON AV.	* TREMONT AVE.	67TH AVE.	SHEPHERD AV.
110TH ST. CATH. PKY.	CLASSON AV.	182ND-183RD STS.	* CONTINENTAL AV.-FOREST HILLS	* EUCLID AV.
103RD ST.	BEDFORD-NOSTRAND AV.	* FORDHAM RD.	75TH AVE.	GRANT AV.
96TH ST.	MYRTLE-WILLOUGHBY AV.	* KINGSBRIDGE RD	* UNION TURNPIKE KEW GARDENS	
86TH ST.	FLUSHING AV.	* BEDFORD PARK BLVD.	VAN WYCK BLVD.	
81ST ST. MUS. OF N.H.	BROADWAY	205TH ST.	SUTPHIN BLVD.	
72ND ST.	METROPOLITAN AVE. GRAND STREET		PARSONS BLVD.	
RT. 102 ÷ 59TH ST.-COL. CIR.	NASSAU AVE.		169TH STREET	
50TH ST.	GREENPOINT AVE.		179TH STREET	
* 42ND ST.	VAN ALST-21ST ST.			
* 34TH ST. PENN. STA.	COURT SQ.			
23RD ST.				
* 14TH ST.	ELY AVE.			
RT. 101 WEST 4TH ST. WASHINGTON SQ.	RT. 104 LEXINGTON AVE.			
SPRING ST.	5TH AVE.			
* CANAL ST.-HOLLAND TUNNEL	* 7TH AVE.			
* CHAMBERS ST. HUDSON TER.				
BROADWAY-NASSAU ST.	RT. 101 50TH ST.			
HIGH ST.-BROOKLYN BRIDGE	* 42ND ST.			
RT. 45 FULTON ST.	* 34TH ST.			
BROAD ST.	23RD ST.			
EIGHTH AVE.	14TH ST.			

CERAMIC DETAIL
Borough Hall IRT Station
Station opened 1908
Brooklyn
The cornucopia, or "horn of plenty"—a popular nineteenth-century symbol of New York's promise of commercial prosperity—shows up in many of Heins & LaFarge's stations. This elaborately designed, three-dimensional ceramic version is typical of the beaux arts approach.

"BH" PLAQUE
Borough Hall IRT Station
Station opened 1908
Brooklyn
Attributed to Grueby Faience Company, Boston, Massachusetts

BOROUGH HALL IRT STATION
Station opened 1908
Brooklyn
Borough Hall is one of the numerous New York City subway stations listed on the National Register of Historic Places.

EIGHTH AVENUE BMT STATION MOSAIC
Station opened 1931
Manhattan
Today's station renovation guidelines encourage new ceramics to
reflect historic precedents. These Eighth Avenue ceramics echo
Vickers's Arts and Crafts approach—small geometric tiles set irregularly
in rectangular patterns—without imitating any specific example.

BUSHWICK-ABERDEEN BMT STATION
Station opened 1928
Brooklyn
This station is part of the 14th Street / Canarsie line, whose ceramics—along with those
of the Flushing line extensions to Times Square and Main Street—fall somewhere
between the Arts and Crafts of the Dual Contracts lines and the Machine Age of the IND
in terms of style. Mirroring trends in the progressive art world of the 1920s, abstract
patterns have replaced the figurative plaques Vickers was using just a decade earlier.

TERRA-COTTA "TULIP" CORNICE SECTION

1904

Removed from Third Avenue / 149th Street IRT station, Bronx

Made by Atlantic Terra Cotta Company, Staten Island and New Jersey

The ornamental border segments in the Third Avenue / 149th Street IRT station come in two varieties, with tulip leaves and stems of different sizes. This piece was removed in 1996 during a major station renovation. The tulip cornices at the Spring Street IRT station come from the same molds used for the Bronx station.

TERRA-COTTA PLAQUE, "3"

Circa 1904

Removed from Third Avenue / 149th Street IRT station, Bronx

Made by the Atlantic Terra Cotta Company, Staten Island and New Jersey

Unlike the smaller art potteries, Atlantic Terra Cotta handled orders for enormous projects, including skyscrapers, and took a more economical approach to production. For the subway commission, the company prepared plaster molds that could be reused. The top scroll on this plaque apparently comes from the same mold as the scrolls on the "S" at Spring Street and the "W" at Worth Street.

TERRA-COTTA PLAQUE, "H"

1908

Removed from Hoyt Street IRT station, Brooklyn

Though similar to plaques in other early IRT stations, this beaux arts station-identification cartouche is a single piece of terra-cotta with cut corners; the "H" is flanked by tulips, rather than the poppies found in other examples.

MOSAIC ROUNDEL, "PAST, PRESENT, FUTURE"
1917
Removed from 137th Street / City College IRT station, Manhattan
At the 137th Street station, a glazed plaque in lavender and
black (the City College colors) reproduced the official City College
seal: three women's faces representing Past, Present and Future
(a translation of the Latin *Respice, Adspice, Prospice*).

137TH STREET / CITY COLLEGE PLAQUE
1917
Removed from 137th Street / City College IRT station, Manhattan
Made by the Atlantic Terra Cotta Company, Staten Island and New Jersey
Heins & LaFarge occasionally took advantage of the mass-production possibilities o[f]
ceramics. This station plaque for 137th Street has two sections: the station number,
usable only at 137th Street, and the cornucopia, which could be used anywhere—an[d]
was, notably at the 86th Street, 145th Street, and 157th Street stations.

CERAMIC DETAIL

Ninth Avenue / New Utrecht BMT Station

Station opened 1916

Brooklyn

This abstract geometric mosaic reflects the subway's basic structural components—vertical columns, horizontal beams, and angled brackets.

CORTLANDT STREET IRT STATION "FERRY" CERAMIC PLAQUE

Station opened 1918

Removed from Cortland Street IRT station, Manhattan

Attributed to Herbert Dole

Manufactured by American Encaustic Tiling Company, Zanesville, Ohio

This plaque—removed during station renovation in the 1970s—shows the Cortlandt Street steam ferry that used to shuttle commuters across the Hudson River between New York and New Jersey. Although it is a single clay tile, the plaque has surface lines filled with grout, mimicking a mosaic of small ceramic pieces—a common effect in Squire J. Vickers's Dual Contracts–era ceramics.

CANAL STREET BMT STATION MOSAIC

Station opened 1918

Removed from Canal Street BMT Station, Manhattan

Designed by Jay Van Everen

Jay Van Everen adapted this design from several nineteenth-century illustrations showing an arched stone bridge and the Stone Bridge Tavern at Canal Street and Broadway in lower Manhattan.

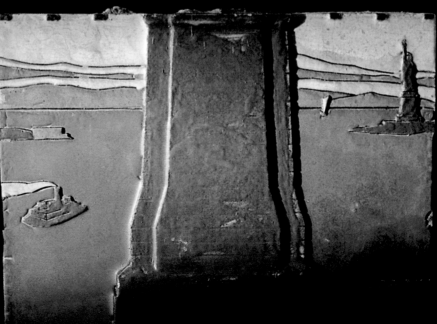

FAIENCE PLAQUE AND DRAWING
"Brooklyn Bridge and New York Harbor"
Drawing 1907; Station opened 1913
Removed from Chambers Street BMT station, Manhattan
Designed by Heins & LaFarge
Designed in 1907, this four-section, T-shaped plaque marks a
transition between the sculptural style of Heins & LaFarge's late
ceramics and Squire J. Vickers's low-relief, faux-mosaic method.

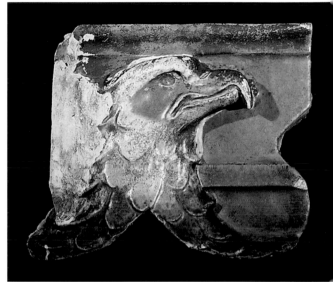

33RD STREET IRT STATION
Station opened 1904
Manhattan
This flat mosaic of an eagle joins the station's more sculptural terra-cotta representations of the national symbol.

TERRA-COTTA SHIELD AND EAGLE HEAD
1904
Removed from 33rd Street IRT station, Manhattan
Made by Grueby Faience Company, Boston, Massachusetts
The terra-cotta eagle that proudly grasps this shield refers to the 71st Regimental Armory that once stood above the 33rd Street station. Similar eagles made their way to the 14th Street and Brooklyn Bridge stations, which is curious—they had no connection to anything nearby. During a 1990s renovation, one of the original eagles served as a model for copies that replaced damaged parts elsewhere at 33rd Street.

REPRODUCTION OF TERRA-COTTA SHIELD AND EAGLE
33rd Street IRT Station
1994
Manhattan
Made by Lisa Portnoff, River City Tile Works, Jersey City, New Jersey
Gift of Lisa Portnoff
Where once upon a time subway ceramics suffered neglect or destruction, today they are carefully restored or reproduced. This copy of an original 1904 Grueby Faience Company eagle from the 33rd Street station was manufactured for a station renovation in the 1990s.

"FRAMING UNION STATION"
14th Street / Union Square IRT Station
Station opened 1904; installation, 1998
Manhattan
MTA Arts for Transit; Mary Miss, artist
Riders can rediscover the architectural history of Union Square station through fragments of
original eagle mosaics and new text and images set in red frames and glass throughout the station.

WALL STREET IRT STATION PLAQUE
Station opened 1904; renovated circa 1970
Manhattan
In the 1970s renovation of Wall Street station,
portions of the 1904 ceramics were retained
but were largely replaced by new materials.

MOSAIC
Canal Street BMT Station
1998
Manhattan
MTA Arts for Transit; Bing Lee, artist
By using tile mosaics with a design suggesting the character of the surrounding Chinatown neighborhood, this contemporary station-identification mosaic reflects the approach of early subway ceramics.

CERAMIC DETAIL "EMPRESS VOYAGE 2.2.1784"
Canal Street BMT Station
1998
Manhattan
MTA Arts for Transit; Bing Lee, artist

STATION CERAMICS
161st Street / Yankee Stadium IND
Station renovated 2002
Bronx
Renovation by MTA Arts for Transit and di Domenico + Partners
A classic Machine Age IND station has been "deconstructed" in this installation.

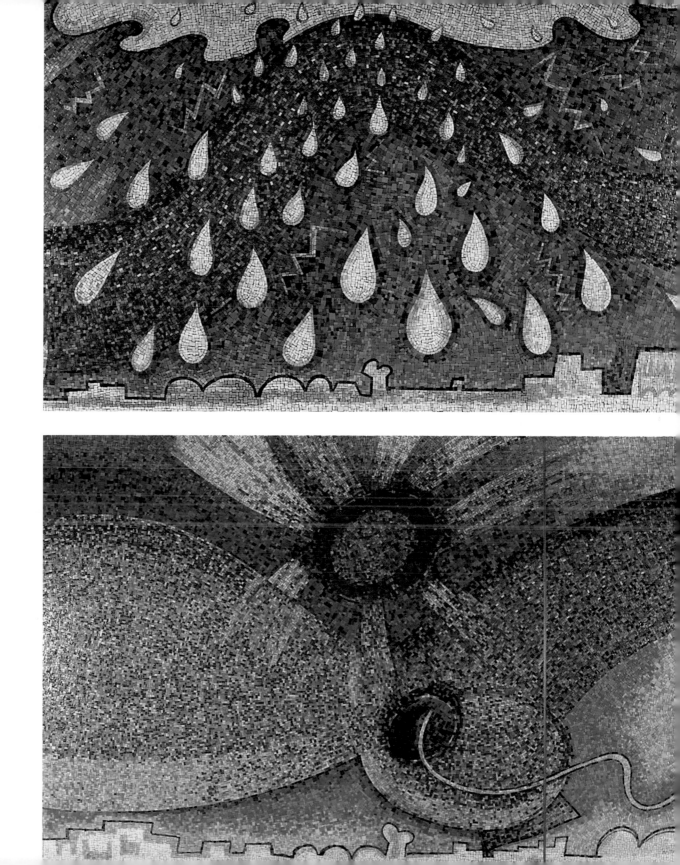

"BLOOMING"
59th Street / Lexington Avenue IRT Station
1996–1998
Manhattan
MTA Arts for Transit; Elizabeth Murray, artist

DETAILS, "STREAM"
23rd Street and Ely IND Station
2001
Queens
MTA Arts for Transit; Elizabeth Murray, artist

METALWORK AND LIGHTING

What is the subway without metal? Steel girders support tunnels and viaducts, cast-iron tubes let trains travel beneath the Harlem and East rivers, and every inch of the system depends upon endless miles of track. Most of the subway's steel is unadorned, even within the stations, suggesting pure industrial power. But much of the metalwork is orna-

THE CAREFUL CONSIDERATION OF EVERY NUT, BOLT, AND SCREW

mental, part and parcel of the designers' overall concept of what the subway should look like. As to lighting, a major source of light in the subways has always been, simply, the sun, certainly on the elevated portions, but also underground, with most of the original stations just one story below street level. Heins & LaFarge lit the showpiece City Hall station with elegant,

leaded-glass skylights in the ceiling vaults. Elsewhere, sidewalk gratings or vault lights—small circles of glass set in concrete slabs—fil-
tered daylight underground. But the subway has always needed
artificial lighting as well, and the electricity that powered the trains
was also harnessed to illuminate the stations.

The subway's grandest displays of ornamental ironwork,
sadly, have almost all disappeared—the 133 cast-iron-and-glass kiosks
that once enclosed the subway's street-level entrances and exits flagged
them for all to see. William Barclay Parsons borrowed the idea directly
from the "kushk" of the Budapest subway. Heins & LaFarge followed
the fanciful Budapest design, with results somewhat reminiscent of
a Victorian greenhouse. Each IRT station originally had separate
entrances and exits, and the kiosk roofs distinguished between them:
a domed roof with cast-iron shingles signaled an entrance, while a

ENTRANCE KIOSK
Circa 1904
City Hall IRT Station, Manhattan
Designed by Heins & LaFarge

METAL EXIT SIGN FROM IRT STATION
Circa 1904–1908
The curved flourishes and serif lettering on this cast-iron sign are
typical beaux arts features.

ELEVATOR-FLOOR INDICATOR
168th Street IRT Station
1906
Manhattan
Because of its location deep underground in the rocky Washington
Heights section of northern Manhattan, the 168th Street IRT station
required passenger elevators. This handsome fixture, with raised serif
letters and an unusually ornamental arrow pointer, reflects the attention
to detail common to all the original IRT stations.

ENTRANCE AT 77TH STREET BMT STATION
January 14, 1916
Brooklyn
While this subway entrance might seem old-fashioned today, its contemporaries would have seen it as a cast-iron harbinger of modernism dropped into a landscape of Victorian single-family, wood-framed houses. The Fourth Avenue line used elaborate versions of Vickers's Arts and Crafts designs, like this entrance whose dual lampposts supporting a sign are found on no other line.

ENTRANCE AT 2 COLUMBUS CIRCLE
59th Street / Columbus Circle Station, Circa 1965, Manhattan
This unique station entrance utilizes the circles of architect Edward Durrell Stone's building at 2 Columbus Circle. The railing has since been removed.

four-sided skylight marked an exit. Within the stations themselves, Heins & LaFarge found further opportunities for decorative metal-work, from curlicue bronze window grilles on ticket booths to curving beaux-arts flourishes on cast-iron exit signs. For electric lighting, the architects looked to traditional models—chandeliers hanging from platform ceilings, lamps within glass globes, and flowery decorative brass wall fixtures holding individual incandescent bulbs.

When Squire J. Vickers took over from Heins & LaFarge, in keeping with his preference for "severe design," he banished beaux arts

gentility from ornamental metalwork, and for lighting relied on simple brass sconces or hexagonal station lamps. "For the sake of sanitation, appearance, and economy in maintenance, surfaces so far as possible are kept plain," he wrote. "Grilles and railings are of plain square bars; doors are of steel and without panels; ticket booths and newsstands are of steel or masonry." Simple as the metalwork might seem, wrote Vickers, "the public would perhaps be astonished to know that every detail of every item (there are 150 items in an average contract) has been the subject of intensive study, that every nut, bolt, screw, and connection of the metalwork has received the most careful consideration."

Despite his insistence on severity, Vickers also brought a taste for geometric patterns to otherwise utilitarian metalwork. In particular, though he "abandoned the old cumbersome kiosk which took up so much of the sidewalk," he still surrounded sidewalk staircases with geometrically patterned metal walls displaying a distinctly Arts and Crafts flair. Twenty years later, while applying the same severity to metalwork in the IND stations, Vickers couldn't avoid the influence of Machine Age modernism. It showed up in the polished, curving, abstract brass sconces; in the choice of new materials like satin-finished aluminum; and in the use of iron zigzags in sidewalk entranceways and ventilator gratings.

After World War II, the subway's iron and brass gave way to the stainless steel and aluminum typical of the International Style, while chandeliers and lightbulbs gave way to endless lines of fluorescent tubes running along the platforms. Both innovations—with the best of progressive intentions—effectively ignored existing subway design. In 1991, however, the plan for station lighting in Prentice, Chan & Olhausen's renovation guidelines provided that, for the first time in decades, lighting would be placed to show off station details like mosaics and structural arches, rather than to hide them.

Today, ornamental metalwork has made a triumphant comeback to the subway system, both in restoration and in new design. The Astor Place station now sports a painstakingly detailed entrance kiosk adapted from the original IRT design. The Arts for Transit program has commissioned bronze sculptures for stations. Some, like Houston Conwill's *The Open Secret* at the 125th Street station (IRT Lexington line), or Harry Roseman's *Subway Wall* at Wall Street (IRT Broadway-Seventh Avenue line), stand on their own as individual works of art. Others, however, also serve a functional purpose. In 1988, at the 23rd Street Station (IRT Lexington line), Valerie Jaudon designed an abstract steel sculpture, *Long Division*, which doubles as a security grille. That sculpture/grille inspired a series of new, standardized railings and grilles throughout the system, designed by sculptor Laura Bradley. Beautiful but also utilitarian, they represent a return to the earliest design philosophy of the subway—just the sort of thing that would have pleased Chief Engineer Parsons.

DETAIL, "A GATHERING,"
Canal Street Station
2000
Manhattan
MTA Arts for Transit; Walter Martin and Paloma Muñoz, artists
A flock of sculpted metal birds alights on the subway's attractive new metal grille.

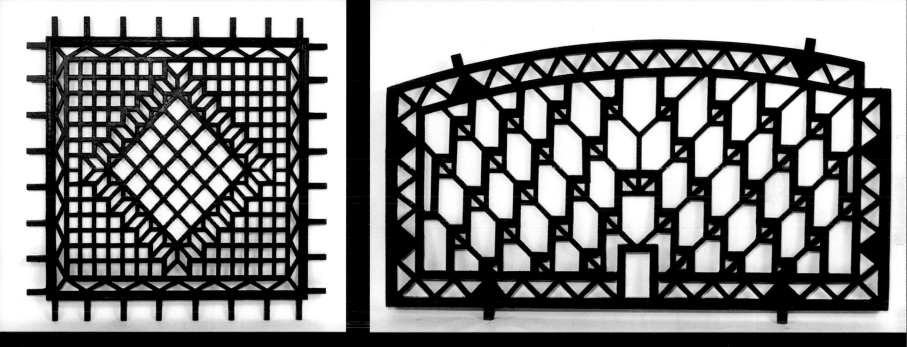

METAL GRILLE
190th Street IND Station
Station opened 1932
Manhattan
Zigzag grilles of the kind more commonly found
on skyscrapers close a rusticated stone arch at
the station entrance to Fort Tryon Park.

CAST-IRON GRILLE
For IND Station Ceiling, Utica Avenue IND Station
Circa 1936
Brooklyn

IND STATION VENT GRILLE
34th Street / Eighth Avenue IND Station
1932
Manhattan
Squire J. Vickers, architect
Cast-iron vent grilles or archway grates in a
distinctive, jazzy Art Deco style provided striking
decorative accents to Vickers's generally austerely
tiled IND station walls. Grilles of the same design
were specified for some IND stations by 1930.

IRT IRON RAILING

Circa 1904–1908

The utilitarian cast-iron pipe railing installed throughout the original IRT system had thin proportions and simple ball finials that fit nicely into both early beaux arts and later Arts and Crafts station designs.

AUTOMATED FARE COLLECTION RAILING

"Medallion"

1989

MTA Arts for Transit; Laura Bradley, artist

Working with MTA Arts for Transit and the Division of Automated Fare Collection (AFC), artist Laura Bradley designed these standard new square tube railings for use in the older IRT and BMT stations—but not in the Machine Age IND stations, for which she created the modernist "Wave" railing.

CAST-IRON EXIT GATE

Circa 1918

Removed from Houston Street IRT Station, Manhattan

When new stations on the Seventh Avenue IRT south of Times Square opened in July 1918—in the days before turnstiles—passengers exited the platforms through heavy cast-iron gates of a geometric Arts and Crafts design. An original set of gates survived at the Houston Street station until its 1994 renovation.

CAST-METAL SIGN
1917
Removed from Park Row IRT Electrical
Substation, Manhattan
Before closing in 1998, Substation
No. 11 played an important role in the
subway's electric power distribution
system. Here and in other substations,
high-voltage alternating current was
converted to lower-voltage direct
current for the subway's third rail. The
prominent cast-metal sign has raised serif
type and a discrete decorative border.

BRONZE PLAQUE
Borough Hall IRT Station
1908
Brooklyn
This plaque commemorates the union of
Brooklyn and Manhattan by subway.

DECORATIVE WINDOW GRILLE
From IRT Ticket Booth
Circa 1904–1908
Until the introduction of turnstiles in the 1920s, passengers bought tickets at paneled oak booths adorned with beautiful beaux arts–inspired bronze grilles.

DETAIL, IRON RAILING
59th Street Powerhouse
1904
Manhattan
Stanford White's massive terra-cotta and brick structure is given a human scale by this whimsical iron railing at sidewalk level.

DETAIL, IRON SIGN
125th Street IRT Station
Station opened 1904
Manhattan
Beaux arts–inspired wrought-iron curlicues bracket a station-identification sign on an elevated platform.

DETAIL, UNTITLED
14th Street / Eighth Avenue IND Station
2000
Manhattan
MTA Arts for Transit; Tom Otterness, artist
Otterness's mischievous cast-bronze sculptures have invaded the
14th Street / Eighth Avenue Station.

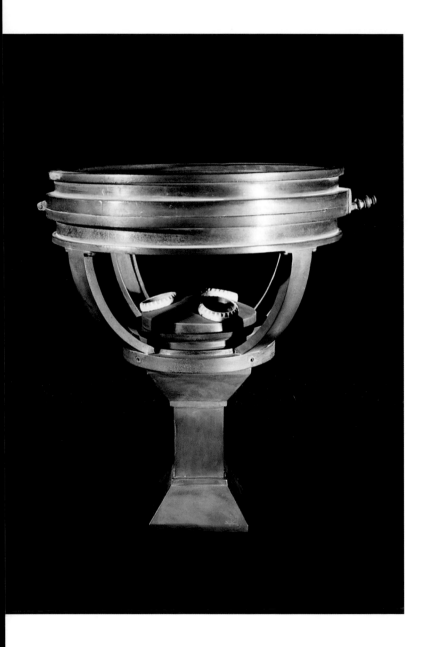

STATION LAMP
Circa 1913
Both short- and long-stemmed versions of these Arts and Crafts–style three-bulb electric brass lamps were designed for stations during the Dual Contracts era.

STATION WALL SCONCE
Circa 1915
Simple geometry and handsome detailing mark this brass electric wall sconce—once commonly found in both IRT and BMT stations—as an Arts and Crafts fixture from the Dual Contracts era.

"TULIP" WALL SCONCE FROM IRT STATION
Circa 1904–1908
What could be more emblematic of beaux arts styling in a subway station than dramatically sculpted flowers cast in brass, designed as electric light fixtures? Heins & LaFarge often used symbols in their subway decoration. Tulips, which symbolized New York City's Dutch colonial past, were used extensively in ceramics as well as other features, such as this wall sconce, during the first phase of IRT subway construction.

INTRODUCTION OF FLUORESCENT LIGHTING
Times Square IRT Station

1957

New York City Transit Promotional Photograph
Courtesy of the New York Transit Museum

This image perfectly captures 1950s thinking
about the subway: smiling, modern New Yorkers
installing bright, energy-efficient modern
lighting in a dark, grimy, outdated environment.
Endless stretches of fluorescent lighting replaced
historic incandescent light fixtures and remained
standard in the system until the 1990s.

DETAIL, FLUORESCENT LIGHTING
Roosevelt Island IND Station
Station opened 1989
Manhattan

ESCALATOR
Roosevelt Island IND Station
Station opened 1989
Manhattan

At nearly 100 feet belowground, Roosevelt Island
is one of the system's deepest stations, making
escalators a necessity for passengers.

STATION ENTRANCE LAMP

Circa 1916

Made for the Brooklyn Rapid Transit Company

From 1913 through the 1920s, octagonal station lamps marked the entrances to many BRT (later, BMT) stations.

GOTHIC-STYLE ENTRANCE LAMP

Circa 1932

Probably removed from Cathedral Parkway IND station, Manhattan

On occasion, Vickers suppressed his Machine Age IND aesthetic to make what he called "a slight Gothic gesture in deference" to nearby landmarks. "When an entrance is planned in or adjacent to one of the parks we co-operate with the Parks Department in an effort to design it in harmony with its surroundings."

STATION ENTRANCE LAMP WITH "M" LOGO

Circa 1980

This subway entrance-marker features the MTA's two-tone "M" logo, designed in 1968. The lamp's blocky form offers a stark contrast to the sculpted cast-iron lampposts of earlier eras.

CONTRACT DRAWING

BRT Station Entrance Lamp

September 6, 1916

Elevation, plan, and section

More than 100 of these specially designed, octagonal iron-and-wire-glass "electroliers" were installed on railing posts at the station stairway entrances on the BRT Broadway / Fourth Avenue lines in both Manhattan and Brooklyn.

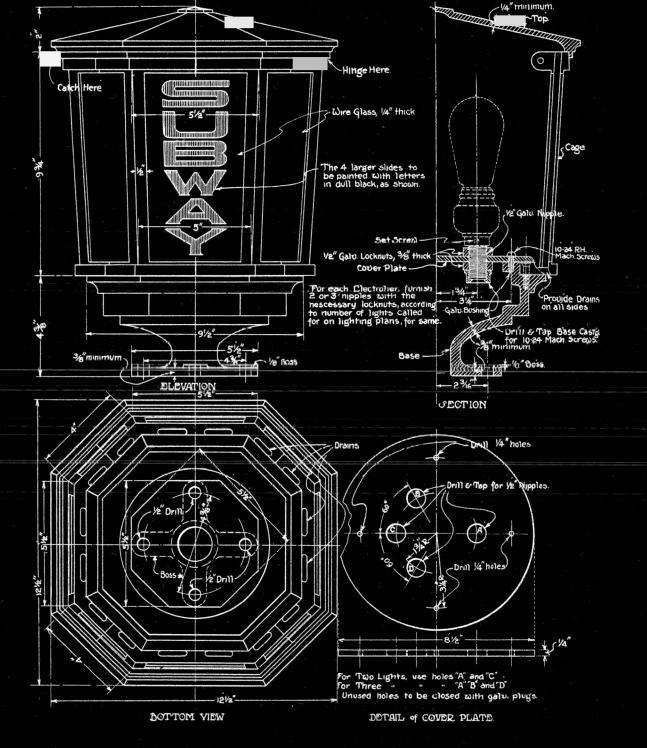

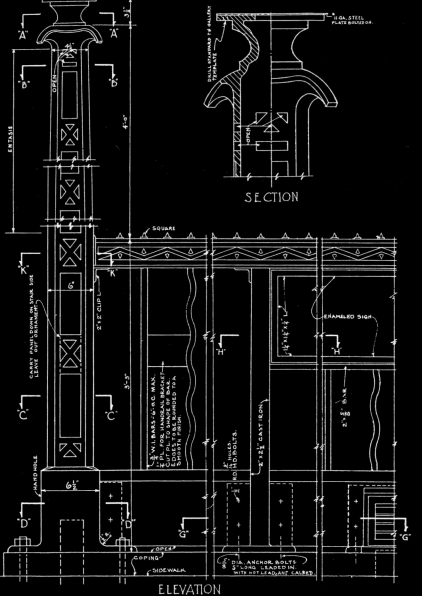

SECTION

ENTASIS

OPEN

SQUARE

2"×12" CLIP L

CARRY PANEL DOWN ON STAIR SIDE
LEAVE OUT ORNAMENT.

ENAMELED SIGN

HAND HOLE

6½"

3"W.I.BARS 6"O.C. MAX.
¼" PL. FOR HANDRAIL BRACKET.
CUT PL.TO SHAPE OF BAR.
EDGES TO BE ROUNDED TO A
SMOOTH FINISH.

2"×5/8" BAR

2"×2½" CAST IRON

2" HOLES
¾" RD. H.D.BOLTS.

4"×4"×¼"

OPEN

COPING

SIDEWALK

5/8" DIA. ANCHOR BOLTS
8" LONG LEADED IN.
WITH HOT LEAD, AND CALKED.

8 GA. STEEL
PLATE BOLTED ON.

DRILL STANDARD T & G GALLERY
TEMPLATE

OPEN

ELEVATION

CONTRACT DRAWING, DETAIL
"KA" IND Station Entrance
Circa 1930
Designed by Herbert Dole
The bridge structure and elegant
geometric patterns of this type of cast-iron
railing and light standard were used for
many IND station entrances, including
that of the old Court Street station in
Brooklyn, which currently houses the
New York Transit Museum.

LAMPPOST, IND STATION
Circa 1932
Designed as an integral part of the
typical IND station entry, this cast-iron
light standard end post is noteworthy
for its crosshatched patterning and
distinctive flanged top.

ENTRY LAMP
Roosevelt Island IND Station
Circa 2000
Manhattan
Green globes, such as this one at
Roosevelt Island, indicate that an entrance
is open twenty-four hours a day.

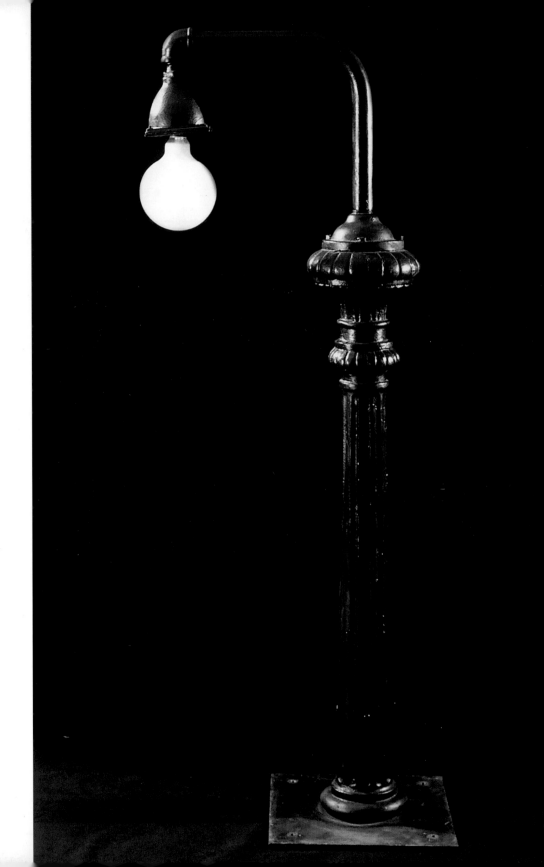

LAMPPOST, IRT ELEVATED STATION
Circa 1904
The economics of mass-production inherent
in cast iron made possible the high level
of detailing on this typically beaux arts
ornamental lamppost, designed specifically
for elevated sections of the IRT in northern
Manhattan and the Bronx.

177TH STREET IRT STATION
Circa 1943
Bronx
The decorative patterns on the ironwork shown
here first appeared along the stairways and
exteriors of Dual Contracts–era IRT elevated
stations in the Bronx, while the lamps show
the beaux arts approach to design typical
of Heins & LaFarge's work. This station, now
known as West Farms Square / East Tremont
Avenue, opened in November 1904.

IRT ELEVATED STATION LIGHTING
Willets Point IRT Station
Station opened 1928; photograph taken 1964
Queens

NINTH AVENUE BMT STATION LIGHTING
Station opened 1915
Brooklyn
Arts and Crafts geometry extends to every element of a Dual Contracts station, including these light standards.

STATION FURNISHINGS

Walk into any subway station and stop at the change booth, buy a snack from a newsstand, make a call at a pay phone, sit down on a bench—all those objects are part of the station's furnishings. Some, like change booths, seating, and clocks, are required for the station to function, and the station's architects sometimes had a hand in choosing them.

THE CITY'S PUBLIC DRAWING ROOMS

Others—pay phones today, and, once upon a time, vending machines and even weight scales—belong to the realm of everyday commercial life; their design reflects the wider material world. But to one degree or another, they have all contributed to the subway's style.

Change booths and seating together form the largest and most visible group of necessary furnishings,

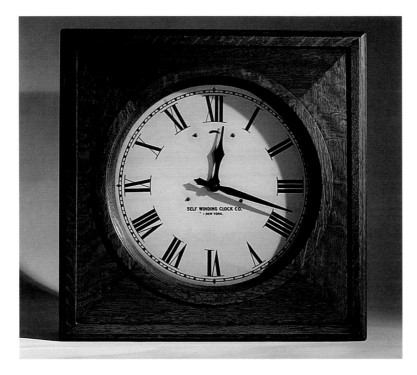

SELF-WINDING CLOCK
Circa 1904–1908
Made by Self-Winding Clock Company Inc., New York
Square, oak-cased, battery-powered pendulum clocks matched the paneled-oak ticket booths and heavy wooden benches of the early IRT stations. They could also be found in many New York City railroad stations, offices, and schools.

STATION BENCH
Circa 1915
Simpler in construction, with thinner members and lines, the new benches of the Dual Contracts–era stations had a lighter appearance than the solid oak Craftsman-style furniture of the earliest IRT stations.

and the history of both follows larger subway trends. Heins & LaFarge's original stations included handsome, solid ticket booths of paneled oak, with ornamental bronze window grilles and fittings. Squire J. Vickers, however, abandoned paneled oak in favor of plain steel as part of his severe approach. The ticket booth eventually gave way to the change booth, and, in 1953, to the token booth, a plain glass-and-metal box whose design reflected an International Style preference for the honest virtues of simplicity and transparency. By the 1970s, the token booth had become a standardized, climate-controlled, prefabricated unit of aluminum, fiberglass, and impact-resistant glass—this last a response to rising crime rates in the subway stations. Today's shiny new change booths, built of prefabricated panels of brushed stainless steel, have a positively squeaky-clean feel to them.

Subway seating, like most of the subway's furnishings, has generally tried to combine stylishness with durability. Somewhat unexpectedly, the original IRT benches departed from the beaux arts sensibilities of their stations. Solid oak, rugged, plain and square, with little decoration other than the grain of the wood, these benches brought an up-to-date version of Arts and Crafts furniture into the system. Sometimes called Mission or Craftsman, such furniture represented the major American contribution to the Arts and Crafts movement. The simple oak station clocks—some incorporated into the ticket booths—also fit the Craftsman mold.

When Vickers took over, he naturally continued to use Arts and Crafts benches but chose a simpler design, lighter and thinner.

The subway's elevated stations got specially designed seating: twin-slatted oak benches fixed back to back, supporting a central wind-screen and station sign rising between and above them and covered by a metal lighting canopy. Slatted backs and seats showed up again in the later, heavy wood IND benches that fit in nicely with the geometric Machine Age look of their stations.

After the 1950s, subway seating turned to plastic, metal, and stone. In many stations, wooden benches gave way to form-fitting, molded fiberglass seats mounted on steel tubing and splayed legs—the subway's version of the famous line of chairs designed by husband-and-wife team Charles and Ray Eames for office-furniture giant Herman Miller, Inc. In the 1960s and '70s, new station designs tried

to integrate seating directly into the overall station look. An in-house design for the new stations of the 63rd Street tunnel project (which opened only in 1989) brought back the slatted look of the 1930s, but for the seat, rather than the back, of a metal bench cantilevered out from a brick wall. Johnson / Burgee's "New Stations Program" prototype at 49th Street included similarly cantilevered, but solid, terrazzo benches projecting out from the glazed orange brick walls. Today's subway benches—mercifully—have given up metal and stone and returned to more comfortable wood. First brought into the system in the mid-1970s, these plain, heavy, angular benches offer a contemporary interpretation of the original IRT Craftsman look.

Most of the commercial furnishings in the subway have disappeared, but surviving photographs still offer an eyeful of twentieth-century popular American commercial culture. Pay phones first found their way into the subway in the late 1920s and early '30s. The IND stations housed them in specially designed white-tiled alcoves. Later, standard wooden phone booths multiplied throughout the system. Both alcoves and booths eventually disappeared from the subway—as they did, sadly, everywhere else in the city—and were replaced with simple column-mounted phones.

Weight scales began turning up on American streets in the 1880s. By the 1930s, the height of their popularity, they numbered more than 750,000. The tall, heavy iron scales—weigh yourself for a penny—brought something of the feel of Coney Island into the subway, where they were often positioned—innocently?—next to the candy machines.

Coin-operated vending machines, the subway's most common commercial fixture, once dispensed everything from chocolate bars to soda to chewing gum. The country's very first vending machine, peddling Adams Tutti-Frutti chewing gum, made its first sale in 1888 on the platform of a New York elevated train. Early vending machines in the subway stations rose out of the floor on spiral iron poles with a modest beaux arts flair. Later models, freestanding or column-mounted, faithfully reflected the commercial styles of the passing decades. By 1972, however, vending machines had not only created hopeless clutter but had also become maintenance headaches, and the MTA banned them.

Despite the ban, a new vending machine thrives today in the subway—the one that sells MetroCards. Created by Antenna Design New York, the MetroCard Vending Machine (MVM) deliberately relies on its looks to entice users. In the words of its designers: "A welcoming appearance eliminates the skepticism of adopting new technology." The MVM is also "hard to scratch and easy to clean." Its shiny appearance deliberately matches the newest change booths, the newest turnstiles, and even the latest subway cars, thereby offering the most consistent approach yet to coordinated subway furnishing design.

SEVENTH AVENUE IND STATION
1970
Manhattan
By the late 1960s, station platforms were often cluttered with vending machines and haphazardly placed furniture, which blocked visibility, created additional refuse, and invited vandalism and accidents. To reduce these problems, most vending machines were removed by the end of the 1970s.

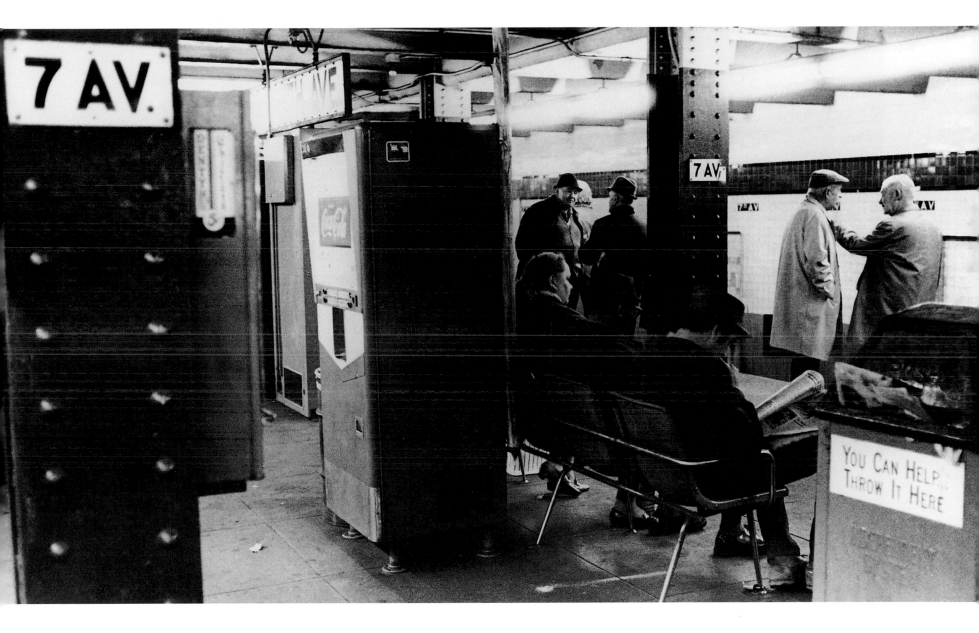

DETAIL, CHEWING GUM VENDING MACHINE
Circa 1940
Removed from the Broadway-Nassau
Street IND station, Manhattan
Vending machines echoed the wider design
trends of their day. This bright red metal,
chrome, and mirrored model has a look
reminiscent of the automobiles and small-
town motels of 1940s America.

VENDING MACHINES AND SCALE
110th Street IRT Station
Circa 1943
Manhattan
Column-mounted vending machines
sold candy and gum to generations of
straphangers. Here, a long, narrow
chocolate-bar dispenser—its rectangular,
Machine Age look vaguely suggestive
of skyscraper design—faces off against
the curves of a nut vending machine
and a weight scale.

STATION BENCH
Circa 1930
This unusual, curved-back bench combines the slatted surfaces of IND benches with the thinner arms, back, and end posts—and the lack of seat dividers and leg-braces—of their Dual Contracts–era predecessors. This, and the following two examples, are found in the New York Transit Museum.

IND STATION BENCH
Circa 1932
For the Machine Age modern underground IND stations, Vickers chose heavy wooden benches with arms, seat dividers, and round-edged, thick-slatted backs and seats.

CONTEMPORARY STATION BENCH
Circa 2000
Manufactured by Theodore Bayer and Sons, West Wyoming, Pennsylvania
Wood benches of this design—with straight solid backs, arms, seat dividers, and inset legs—were first installed in some stations in the mid-1970s. By the 1990s, they had become the standard seating furniture not only in the subway system, but also in many other city public transportation facilities, such as the Staten Island Ferry terminals.

LARIAT SEAT LOOPS
33rd Street IRT Station
Station opened 1904; artwork installed 1996
Manhattan
MTA Arts for Transit; James Garvey, artist
These column-mounted bronze railings look like
sculpture but also function as seating.

STATION BENCH
49th Street BMT Station
1973
Manhattan
Philip Johnson and John Burgee, architects
Simple and elegant, this cantilevered, cast-terrazzo
bench seems to grow organically from the wall,
making it an integral part of the station's
International Style makeover.

BENCHES
161st Street / Yankee Stadium IND Station
Station renovated 2002
Bronx
Renovation by MTA and di Domenico + Partners

BENCH
Roosevelt Island Station
Station opened 1989
Manhattan
Roosevelt Island Station is distinctive because of
the curved walls and the metal ceiling.

BENCH
21st Street / Queensbridge IND Station
Station opened October 29, 1989
Queens

ELEVATED SUBWAY PLATFORM BENCH
Queensboro Plaza BMT Station
Circa 2000; based on design circa 1916
Queens
Vickers's Arts and Crafts design ingeniously
incorporates seating, windscreen, signage,
and lighting. The original benches were
designed and constructed without seat dividers.

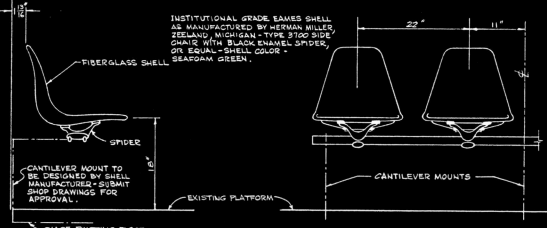

STANDARD POST-WAR SEATING
West Fourth Street IND Station
Design Circa 1960
Manhattan
Turquoise molded-fiberglass seats, supported by splayed tubular metal legs, pay homage to the optimistic, space-age furniture design of the 1960s. The chairs have long since vanished from the subway system.

DRAWING DETAIL
"Eames Shell" Station Seats—Contract C-193
1968
Designed by Charles Eames
Manufactured by Herman Miller
In 1969, office-furniture manufacturer Herman Miller produced a subway version of the acclaimed "Eames Shell," a biomorphically shaped fiberglass chair supported on simple metal mounts. Introduced in the Prospect Avenue station in Brooklyn, as well as stations on the BMT-division Fourth Avenue line, the Eames Shells fell victim to vandalism in the 1970s and soon disappeared from the system.

BENCHES
Jamaica / Van Wyck IND Station
Station opened 1989
Queens
The designers of the Jamaica / Van Wyck station—one of the newest in the subway system—chose bright red, cast-molded polyurethane seating to complement the station's lively, modern design.

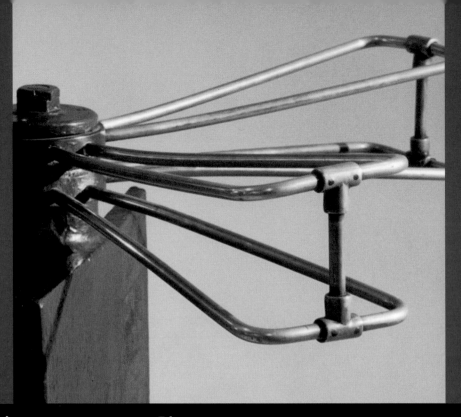

FARE COLLECTION

The subway's turnstiles, besides being a given in the lives of most New Yorkers, handily illustrate the modern American tension between art and engineering, and the resulting emergence of the profession of industrial design. The earliest models showed little interest in aesthetic qualities; they simply performed their functions as efficiently as possible, like

IN 1904, A RIDE ON THE SUBWAY COST A NICKEL

any other piece of machinery. Some—notably the revolving cage "High Entrance Turnstile" (familiarly known as the "Iron Maiden")—owed their design strictly to the need to keep out fare-beaters. Neither Parsons nor his architects apparently gave much thought to the turnstiles. Only in the 1930s did manufacturers really begin to treat them as objects of

design, turning an eye to their overall appearance beyond strictly functional requirements.

Subway fare-collection technology developed in stages, mirroring the general transformation of American industry. Passengers paid their fare using, first, a paper ticket, then a coin, then a metal token, and finally a plastic card. The system collected those fares first by hand, then by a mechanical device, then by an electric device, and finally by computer.

In 1904, a ride on the subway cost a nickel. Passengers handed five cents to a clerk in a ticket booth, received a paper ticket, and then handed the ticket to a second clerk operating a ticket-chopper. A solid piece of furniture in paneled oak with brass fixtures, the ticket-chopper nicely matched its contemporary ticket booth and would have been at home in any turn-of-the-century living room—except for the glass enclosure at the top, into which the clerk dropped the ticket, and the machinery inside that chopped the ticket to bits.

Following World War I, major inflation, combined with political reluctance to raise the nickel fare, led to the introduction of the "Passimeter," an automatic coin-fed turnstile, which cut costs by eliminating the ticket taker. In one early model, the "Coinpassor," passengers dropped a nickel in a slot and pushed the turnstile, thereby setting in motion an internal mechanism that measured the coin (to verify its value) before unlocking the turnstile arms. Before long, an electric version debuted on the IRT, drawing its power from the same third rail

NICKEL
1920–1948

DIME
1948–1953

VAULTING, TILES, AND TICKET BOOTH
City Hall IRT Station
1904
Manhattan
Planned as the grand gateway to the new subway system, the IRT's City Hall Station offered New Yorkers the most beautiful subway station the city would ever know—until it closed in 1945. Its lush beaux arts design included an arched, domed roof of Guastavino tiles; amethyst glass vault lights; and radiant chandeliers. The ticket booth—long since demolished—boasted dark wood, elegant wainscoting, recessed panels, playful metalwork, and elaborate detail.

TICKET CHOPPERS AND ATTENDANT
South Ferry IRT Station
1908
Manhattan

CONSTRUCTION DRAWING
IRT Ticket Chopper
Circa 1900
Made by Ingersoll-Sergeant Drill Company
The ticket chopper, or "ticket canceling box," came to the subway from the city's elevated rail system, where it had first appeared in the 1870s or 1880s. Passengers dropped their tickets into the box through a slot at the top; an attendant watched the ticket through a glass panel, and then shredded it mechanically. The construction drawing shows how the handle engaged the shredding mechanism.

IRT TICKET CHOPPER
Patented November 6, 1894
Made by Ingersoll-Rand Company, New York, for the IRT
The boxy, paneled-oak ticket chopper shares the Arts and Crafts look of other early IRT furnishings

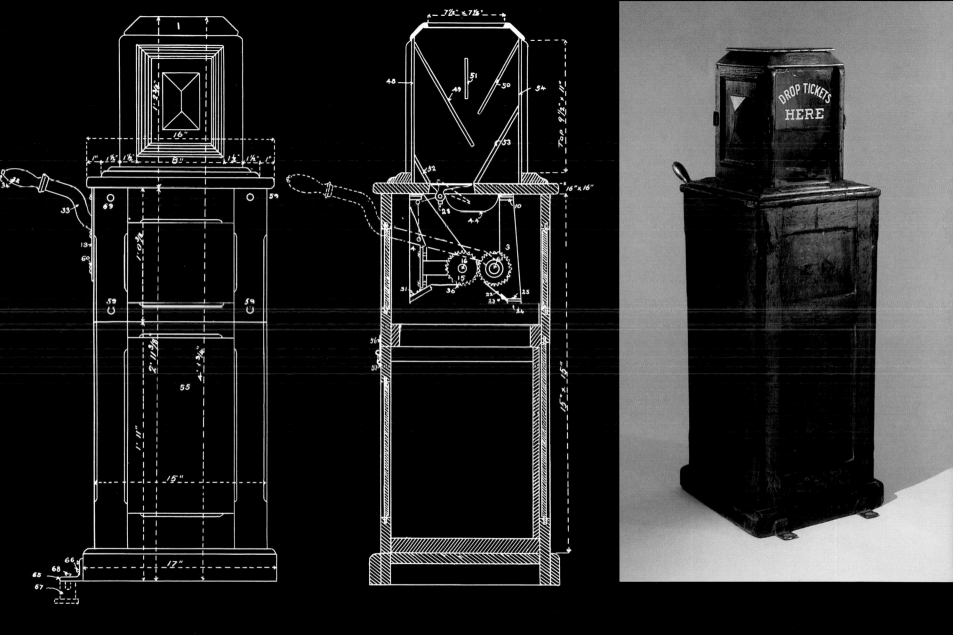

as the trains. Early models in heavy cast iron gave way to lighter versions in sheet steel, but the general look, with four heavy rotating wood paddles, stayed unchanged—utilitarian, efficient, and unremarkable.

And then, in 1932, the lowly fare-collecting machine met up with an industrial designer. What Henry Dreyfus did for the New York Central Railroad's 20th Century Limited, and Raymond Loewy did for the Greyhound bus, John Vassos did for the subway turnstile—he brought it into the age of streamlining. Inextricably bound up with Machine Age optimism, streamlining's sweeping curves, rounded corners, and horizontal speed lines seemed to promise a more prosperous future through advances in modern industry. Depression-era manufacturers saw industrial design generally and streamlining in particular as a marketing tool that could increase sales. Designers like Loewy, Dreyfus, Norman Bel Geddes, and Russel Wright found fame and fortune streamlining everything from toasters and radios to automobiles and airplanes. Vassos, a freelance designer who had studied at the Art Students League, brought streamlining to RCA radio cabinets and Coca-Cola soda fountain dispensers. For the Perey Turnstile Company, he redesigned the Coinpassor, simplifying it, reducing the number of materials, and giving it a sleek, modern finish with rounded ends, incised metallic lines along its top, and horizontal metal strips wrapped around its upper edges. While such apparently superfluous details might have seemed a costly luxury for a modest

FOUR-ARM BMT COINPASSOR
1920–1925
Made by Perey Manufacturing Company, New York
Early automated turnstiles included this completely mechanical BMT Coinpassor. Quieter and easier to maintain than electric turnstiles, the Coinpassor became a mainstay of the entire system.

ROUND-END KOMPAK MODEL 97
1946
Made by Perey Manufacturing Company, New York
Courtesy of the New York Transit Museum Archive
The Perey Round-End Kompak model 97 is a refinement of an earlier turnstile. Originally, the machines were designed with a glass-windowed slug spotter, but the windows were covered over with metal plates after repeated vandalism.

KOMPAK COINPASSOR, MODEL 107
1968
Made by Perey Manufacturing Company, New York
The mechanics of this Perey Kompak Coinpassor are similar to those of previous Kompak models. Building on the success of model 97, model 107 became the most common turnstile in the system throughout the 1970s and into the 1980s. While a full-flush floor supported the earlier Kompaks, this model has a pedestal at either end to facilitate cleaning.

AFC TURNSTILES
72nd Street IRT Station, Introduced 1992, Manhattan
Cubic Transport Systems, Inc.
The Automatic Fare Card (AFC) turnstile is the system's most recent model. Besides the standard token slot, each turnstile also has a magnetic fare card reader, which subtracts fares from the card and calculates the remaining value.

Depression-era piece of machinery, according to a 1934 write-up in *Fortune* magazine, Vassos's improved design actually lowered the turnstile's cost, while its spiffy look increased sales by 25 percent. The new Perey model remained the subway standard for decades.

The nickel fare survived until 1948, when it finally jumped to a dime. When the fare increased again, in 1953, to fifteen cents, Perey redesigned the Coinpassor to accept not a coin but a subway token—a New York City icon for half a century. The Perey Company continued to provide Coinpassors for the subway, tweaking its design here and there, until 1992, when the computer revolution shook up the subway system. In that year, the MTA introduced the Automatic Fare Card (AFC) turnstile equipped to read a new magnetic fare card, better known as a MetroCard.

The AFC turnstile, manufactured by Cubic Transport Systems, Inc., is shiny, metallic, high-tech, and utterly functional. The turnstile's futuristic geometry, in fact, is meant primarily to frustrate fare-beaters; its slanted sides discourage leaping over the turnstile, while its reduced width (just fifteen inches) discourages crawling beneath it. The AFC even comes with an updated version of the Iron Maiden, the HEET (High Entrance/Exit Turnstile), a MetroCard-reading revolving cage that functions as both entrance and exit. The system's shiny design seems to offer a better future through improved technology, and that, after all, has always been the subway's underlying promise.

BRT TURNSTILE
Circa 1915
Made by Perey Manufacturing Company, New York
A turnstile attendant operated this early BRT model by pressing a pedal to release the arm and let passengers through. During off-peak hours, the ticket booth attendant could operate the turnstile by pulling a rope connected to a lever just above the pedal. Early BRT models had arms of soldered brass tubing; later models used more durable cast aluminum. Both versions were surprisingly lightweight, simple, and elegant in design—especially in comparison to the bulky, wood-paddled IRT and BMT models of the 1920s and 1930s.

NO-FARE TURNSTILE
Circa 1932
Designed by John Vassos
Made by Perey Manufacturing Company, New York
Industrial designer John Vassos (1898–1985) revolutionized turnstile design with this streamlined version of the early 1930s. Vassos replaced the four bulky wood paddles of earlier models with three slanted tubular-metal arms and gave it a simply curved steel-and-enamel base.

AFC TURNSTILES
Introduced 1992
Cubic Transport Systems, Inc.

TOKEN BOOTH AND TURNSTILES
Interior of Control House at South Ferry
IRT Station
June 2, 1960
Manhattan
The 1960 rebuilding of the 1905 South
Ferry station included the installation of a
new metal-and-glass token booth. This
photograph emphasizes the transparency
of the new control house, an airy
International Style pavilion of plate glass
with open aluminum railings.

MODEL, PROTOTYPE AGENT BOOTH
Christopher Street IRT Station
Circa 1994
Made by Todd Architectural Models, Somerville, New Jersey
Project Designed by MTA New York City Transit
This prototype—a simple metal-and-glass agent
booth with a controlled environment—served as the
model for many booths of the 1990s. The introduction
of the MetroCard has changed the role of the booth
agent—who now devotes less time to selling fares
and more to information and security duties—so this
booth design will eventually be replaced.

TOKEN VENDING MACHINE
Circa 1960

TOKEN VENDING MACHINES
Times Square IRT Station
Circa 1960
Manhattan

TOKEN VENDING MACHINE
Circa 1986

Token photographs by Steven Williams

SMALL Y-CUT TOKEN
1953–1970

QUARTER-SIZED Y-CUT TOKEN
1970–1980

QUARTER-SIZED SOLID TOKEN
1980–1986

BULL'S-EYE TOKEN
1986–1995

FIVE BOROUGH TOKEN
1995–2003

METROCARDS

1994 and 1997

The current gold-colored MetroCard made its appearance in 1997, with the conversion of the entire subway to automated fare collection. The original MetroCard, however—introduced in a limited number of stations in 1994—had a blue background and gold lettering.

METROCARD AUTOMATIC VENDING MACHINES

1997 and 1999

Designed by Antenna Design New York Inc.

In order to integrate new technology, such as automatic fare collection and vending, into public spaces in the subway system, the fixtures and equipment are designed and placed according to carefully established guidelines. The MetroCard Automatic Vending Machine (1997) was designed to be easily understood and used. The look of the machine—intended to fit into the subway station context by reflecting existing materials and colors—relates to the tasks performed: green for money (in) and yellow for MetroCard (out). The compact MetroCard Express Machine (1999) offers the same design features but is smaller because it has no cash function or mechanism.

Three separate systems, dozens of lines, hundreds of stations where local, express and shuttle trains share platforms and tracks—the subway's complexity is astounding. Yet somehow, millions of passengers routinely find their way through the labyrinthine system. That they do so is a testament to the power of graphic design—a discipline whose name hadn't even

A WAY OUT OF THE LABYRINTH

been coined when the IRT began service in 1904, but which grew into a system of signage, lettering, color codes, and maps that brought clarity, unity, and order to the most daunting system.

Heins & LaFarge created the subway's earliest graphics by incorporating station names into their ornamental ceramics. The architects intended each

MOSAIC SIGN
"Men," Cortlandt Street IRT Station
Circa 1918
Manhattan
This Dual Contracts–era mosaic restroom sign has rich color variations in its tile glazes.

RENDERING
IND Ceramic Ornamentation
February 2, 1934
Produced to indicate the color details of wall tile, this watercolor demonstrates the clean geometry and stark, sans-serif typeface of Machine Age design. The signage in the drawing suggests that it wasn't meant to illustrate any specific station but just to show possibilities of color and typeface.

station to look distinct from the next, so their graphics varied from station to station, and even within stations. They approached lettering as a decorative element and used several fonts—the designs of the individual letters. Like the Victorians in general, who responded to a nineteenth-century explosion of new fonts by mixing and matching, Heins & LaFarge used both serif fonts (letters with fine lines finishing off the main strokes) and sans serif (no such fine lines), all uppercase. In general, they preferred serif lettering for sculptural faience or terra-cotta plaques like the flowery "BH" monogram at Brooklyn Borough Hall and sans serif for flat surfaces, whether ceramic or glass tile mosaics. They also hung large, illuminated porcelain-enamel signs over the express platforms, using black type on a white background and painted station names on the round cast-iron columns.

In his earliest work, Squire J. Vickers continued Heins & LaFarge's practice of writing station names in glass tiles on the walls but, unlike his predecessors, he used serif lettering almost exclusively, perhaps because sans serif block letters suggested something of the machine, while serif letters seemed individually crafted. Vickers also greatly expanded the use of large signs hanging from ceilings or mounted on columns. Signs began to multiply as the rivals IRT and BMT erected more and more of them to distinguish their respective lines—the IRT using white type on a cobalt blue background, the BMT red and white type on a green background.

Even as he expanded the use of directional signs, Vickers noticed that passengers would still "now and then complain that they

FT. HAMIL

7ᵗʰ AVE. STATION

7ᵗʰ AV

← GREENW

7ᵗʰ AVE.

FT. HAMILTON PKWY

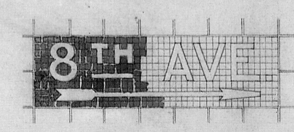

8ᵗʰ AVE

GREENWOOD AVE.

TO MANHATTAN

are unable to find the station name." Hence his new approach for the IND, a decade later, incorporating the alternating color-coded strips of tile along the platform walls. He also changed his typography in response to European developments. Modernist European typography preferred the bold look of the sans-serif, and embraced new fonts with names like "Futura." In London, the Underground adopted a comprehensive graphic look that included—besides the ubiquitous symbol of a blue bar across a red circle—a specially designed geometric "Railway Type." Hardly immune to such influences, Vickers abandoned his earlier lettering for the Modernist look, taking pains to specify the details, black type on white porcelain enamel, in the IND contract documents.

In the decades that followed, directional signs continued to multiply, building up to a visual overload. By the 1950s, New York City had become a world center for art, including graphic design, but the subway had yet to benefit. In 1957, graphic designer George Salomon approached the Transit Authority and offered to unify the subway's graphics and bring order to what had become chaos and clutter. Calling his proposal "Out of the Labyrinth," Salomon declared that "the subway system has now reached a point where only an expert can find his way around it." He proposed "to transform the subway network from a bewildering puzzle into an intelligible, easily remembered system." Salomon's strategy included standardization of all the system's design elements—signs, maps, train indicators—but in the end, the Transit Authority used only his map. Not until the early 1970s did the subway system adopt the

SIGNAGE

59th Street IRT Station, Circa 1965, Manhattan
The gradual buildup of signs over the decades created visual chaos and confusion for passengers—a crisis that finally, in the late 1960s, led to the complete overhaul and standardization of subway signage and graphics.

IND STATION SIGN

"No Smoking / Spitting," Circa 1937
Made by Nelke-Porcelain Metals, New York
Public health in the crowded underground conditions of the subway had been a matter of citywide concern, even before the opening of the original IRT system. In an era before effective treatments were available for tuberculosis or influenza, signs prohibiting smoking and spitting were installed in subway stations from the very beginning. Vickers's plans for the IND specified the design and placement of these standardized signs.

The illustration shows three examples of letter spacing.
The first line is an example of space units found between letters of opposed and similar visual character.

The second and third lines show the space unit counts found in typical words used in the subway system. The chart on page 10 shows all possible letter and number combinations and their space unit counts. The size and positions of the space units in relation to the three alphabet sizes are found on pages 88-170.

odvepnlry

1 1 -1 2 2 3 3 0

Uptown

3 0 0 -1 1

Broadway

2 0 1 2 1 -1 -1

The following examples show the basic categories of signs. All the text for Identification, Direction and Information signage will appear in black on a white background. Discs will always be colored with white numerals or letters. Directional arrows will be black on a white background.

To avoid visual confusion and clutter only the standard sign plates should be used for each category of sign. Any other device like painting on tiles, walls, light fixtures, etc. is a violation of the standards.

3   →   For 23 St & 14 St
Mon-Fri
6:50 am to 10:05 am
3:30 pm to 6:55 pm
Take any train to 34 St
Change for ●

1

Downtown & Brooklyn

2

Broadway Nassau

3

Top illustration is a typical side-destination sign on the outside of the train. Bottom illustration is a typical line map inside the train.

The Outside Identification Sign
The traveler standing on the platform will view the line identification (E in white on colored background) and the names of the terminal stations at each end of the line in white on a black background. This is an insert on the side of the train facing the traveler on the platform. For the production of the terminal names use 4¼" type (see pages 152-167). This type must be reduced proportionally to the 1" signs. See dimensions on illustration below.

The Inside Line Map
The passenger in the train will view a color

coded line map on a white background (the color is indicated below in grey. Discs and train letters are black). This map informs him about: the line; the terminal stations; the transfer points and transfer lines. For better distinction between type showing express stops and local stops we have chosen 48 pt. Standard medium and light. Dimensions and specifications are shown in examples below.

Colors and Production
The line strip and the line identification discs are color coded, see and match color swatches on pages: 46-54.
For reproduction of the discs see pages 35-44.

E ## 179 Street
Euclid Avenue

10½" x 53"

E ─────────────

169 St   local   express

Par...

F

1 2 3 4 5 6
7 8 A AA B CC
D E EE F GG HH
KK LL M N QB OJ
RR SS

comprehensive graphic program designed by Massimo Vignelli, whose style still rules the subways.

Vignelli's work reflected two major trends, one European in origin and one American. From Europe came the International Typographic Style, or "Swiss design." Characterized by sans serif fonts, with type organized asymmetrically along mathematical grids, the style seemed to offer a more universal, scientific approach to typography. One new Swiss font—unusually clear and easy on the eye—became the darling of the international design world: "Helvetica," after the Latin name for Switzerland. Meanwhile, America's business world had developed a new passion for graphic "corporate identity." Unimark, a leader in the field, designed dynamic logos and graphics for clients including Alcoa, Ford, and Xerox. Vignelli, head of Unimark's New York office, would design a new corporate identity for the MTA, one that would rely heavily on the mathematical grid and on Helvetica.

In 1970, Vignelli created a graphics standards manual for the subway that divided signs into three categories—station identification, directions, and information—and determined characteristics to distinguish each from the other. The manual specified every conceivable signage and typographic detail, exclusively in Helvetica, down to letter and word spacing and "construction of the arrow." The original plan called for black type on a white background, but that quickly changed to white type on a black background because it seemed easier to read.

One of Vignelli's greatest successes brought order out of the chaos of subway line names and numbers. The subway historically identified each line in several ways; so the "1" train, the Broadway/

Selections from
NEW YORK CITY TRANSIT AUTHORITY GRAPHICS STANDARDS MANUAL
1970
Designed by Unimark International, New York

Seventh Avenue local, and the IRT West Side local are all the same line. Vignelli focused on the letter and number identifications, assigned a colored circle to each one, and insisted that signs always list them in alphabetical and numerical order. Without actually renaming the lines after their colors (as in Boston), the system built up a subconscious connection between, say, a blue circle and the Eighth Avenue lines (A, C, E).

To avoid confusion, Vignelli insisted on replacing all existing signage with the new version. The older signs have largely disappeared, except, of course, for the names built into the walls as glass tiles and ceramics. Today, Heins & LaFarge's decorative lettering faces off against Vignelli's uniform Helvetica—and together they guide New Yorkers not just through the subway, but also through its graphic history.

IND/BMT SUBWAY CAR-FRONT ROUTE ROLL CURTAIN
Circa 1970
Made by Trans-Lite, Inc., Milford, Connecticut
The Unimark/Vignelli graphics standards introduced a spectrum of bright colors into the dark world of the subway. Nine hues were selected for line identification signage, many in the same Day-Glo colors then being used by Madison Avenue and the fashion industry. This route sign for the front of the subway car replaced an earlier black-and-white version on R-16 cars.

STATION SIGNAGE
161st Street and River Avenue, Yankee Stadium, Bronx
Circa 1970
During the 1960s and 1970s, the Transit Authority installed enormous panels with oversized graphics in many stations. Some of the panels displayed historic images, others—like the one pictured here at Yankee Stadium—had the station's name.

ILLUMINATED BOX ENTRANCE SIGN WITH SEA HORSES
Circa 1927
From the Graybar Building, former subway entrance at
Lexington Avenue and 43rd Street
This dramatic, finely-crafted sign features an unusual maritime
motif related to design elements on architects Sloan & Robertson's
Graybar (originally, Eastern Offices) Building.

STATION ENTRANCE LAMP
IND Fourth Avenue / Ninth Street Viaduct
1933
Brooklyn
Designed by Frank T. Fellner
The geometric motif of this cast-aluminum lamp was a continuation of the "jazz-age"
brickwork that distinguishes this Art Deco example of Squire J. Vickers's work for the IND.

STATION ENTRANCE AT MUNICIPAL BUILDING
Chambers Street IRT Station
Station opened 1918
Manhattan

STATION FINISH CONTRACT DRAWING
IND Subway Signpost
November 9, 1931
Squire J. Vickers, architect; Deisler and Caradonna, draftsmen
Contract documents contained detailed drawings for special fixtures such as this standing bronze-plated illuminated subway entrance sign designed for sections of the IND, including the area in Brooklyn between the Transit Museum's Court Street station and the Clinton-Washington Avenue station on the A and C lines.

"SUBWAY" SIGN AND LIGHT
190th Street IND Station
Station opened 1932
Manhattan
A Paris Metro–inspired illuminated sidewalk stanchion calls attention to the station entrance carved into the rock outcropping in Fort Tryon Park. Such stanchions were also found in downtown and midtown Manhattan when entrances were incorporated into the bases of office buildings.

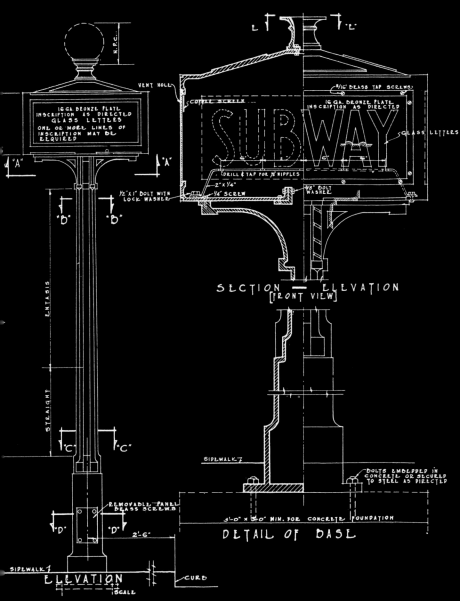

INSCRIPTION AS DIRECTED
GLASS LETTERS
ONE OR MORE LINES OF
INSCRIPTION MAY BE
REQUIRED

16 GA. BRONZE PLATE

VENT HOLE

"A"

"A"

½"x 1" BOLT WITH
LOCK WASHER

"D"

"D"

ENTASIS

STRAIGHT

"C"

"C"

REMOVABLE PANEL
BRASS SCREWS

"D"

"D"

2'-6"

SIDEWALK

ELEVATION
⅛ SCALE

CURB

COPER SCREW

⁵⁄₁₆" BRASS TAP SCREWS

16 GA. BRONZE PLATE
INSCRIPTION AS DIRECTED

GLASS LETTERS

SUBWAY

DRILL & TAP FOR ⅛" NIPPLES

2"x ¼"

⅛" BOLT
WASHER

¼" SCREW

SECTION — ELEVATION
[FRONT VIEW]

SIDEWALK

BOLTS EMBEDDED IN
CONCRETE OR SECURED
TO STEEL AS DIRECTED

3'-0" x 3'-0" MIN. FOR CONCRETE FOUNDATION

DETAIL OF BASE

INTERBOROUGH
RAPID TRANSIT CO.
UPTOWN TO WOODLAWN.
DOWNTOWN VIA LEX. AND 4TH AV.
TO GRAND CENTRAL.
CITY HALL, SOUTH FERRY AND BROOKLYN.
CHANGE AT 149TH ST. FOR TIMES SQ., PENN. STATION.
SOUTH FERRY, WALL STREET AND BROOKLYN
VIA BROADWAY AND 7TH AVENUE.
TO SO. FERRY VIA 6TH AND 9TH AVE. ELEVATED.

8TH AVENUE
INDEPENDENT SUBWAY SYSTEM
UPTOWN TO 207TH ST.
THE BRONX AND QUEENS
TO BROOKLYN

IRT ENTRANCE SIGN
"Interborough Rapid Transit Co. /
Uptown to Woodlawn"
Circa 1918
Made by Nelke Signs, New York
For destination and entrance signs, the IRT used cobalt blue porcelain enamel metal plaques with white lettering. Used sparingly from 1904 to 1908, IRT signage later multiplied when the system expanded and the rival BRT subway opened.

IND ENTRANCE SIGN
"8th Avenue / Independent Subway System /
Uptown to 207th St."
Circa 1932
Made by Baltimore Enamel Company, New York
For IND entrance signs, Vickers specified dark green porcelain enamel plaques with white sans-serif uppercase type.

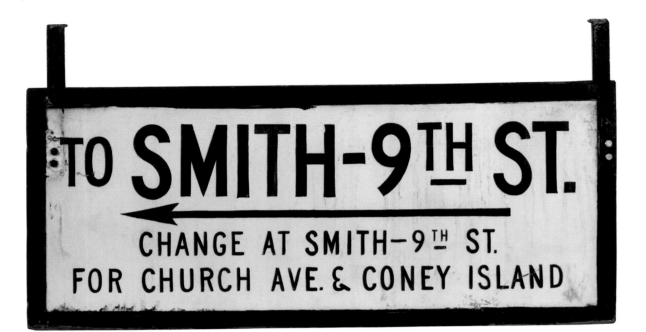

IND STATION DIRECTIONAL SIGN

"To Smith-9th St."

Circa 1933

Brooklyn, Smith-Ninth Street Station

IND metal directional
signs—suspended from the
ceiling—typically used black type
on a white background.

SIGN

"To Downtown Trains"

Circa 1920

*Made by Nelke Veribrite Signs,
New York*

The long, low proportions of this
sign worked well in passageways and
on platforms with little headroom.

IND STATION SIGN

"To All Trains"

Circa 1930

*Made by Baltimore Enamel Company,
New York*

VAN WYCK

KINGS-BRDG.

BALTO. ENAMEL 200 FIFTH AVE. NY CS-7

MOSAIC COLUMN MARKER

"Bushwick Aberdeen," Bushwick-Aberdeen BMT Station

Station opened December 14, 1928

Brooklyn

Most column markers are enameled metal signs with

black type on a white background, but the unusual

IND COLUMN MARKER SIGNS

"Van Wyck" and "Kings-brdg."

1937

Queens, Van Wyck Boulevard IND Station, and Bronx, Kingsbridge Road IND Station

Made by Nelke-Porcelain Metals, New York and Baltimore Enamel Company, New York

One of Vickers's innovations for the IND system was to place small square or rectangular station

↑ Exit New York Coliseum

Downtown & Bklyn via 8 Av Local **E** **To: World Trade Center all times**

STATION EXIT SIGN
"Exit / New York Coliseum"
59th Street / Columbus Circle Station
Circa 1975
Manhattan
The Unimark graphics system uses standardized modules that can be assembled—according to strict design rules—into composite directional, identification, or information signs.

IND STATION PLATFORM DIRECTIONAL SIGN
"Downtown & Bklyn via 8 Av Local"
Circa 1975
The Unimark / Vignelli graphics standards originally specified that all signs would have black lettering on a white ground. These fields were reversed in the early 1970s, when it was determined that white lettering on black was more legible for passengers.

SIGNAGE AND AFC TURNSTILES
Roosevelt Island IND Station
Station opened 1989
Manhattan

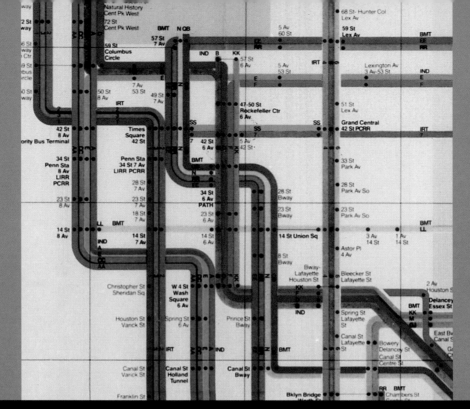

ROUTE AND SYSTEM MAPS

"You can take the A train," says Billy Strayhorn's song, but only if you know where it's going. The subway map must be far and away the most frequently consulted of any map of the city—or of any in the city's history. Today's version, a marvel of clarity and order considering the mass of information it holds, supercedes a century's worth of maps that have swung

back and forth between Chief Engineer Parsons' twin goals of beauty and utility. Those many versions also reflect the subway's evolution from separate systems to unification, as well as the relationship between subway geography and city geography.

The subway map-as-objet d'art goes back to 1904, when August Belmont, financier of the IRT,

commissioned a sterling silver Tiffany tray engraved with a map of the original route. Several years passed before the IRT produced a paper version for everyday use, leaving that job to local department stores and hotels. When the company finally issued its first maps, it followed a century-long tradition of portraying New York's streets as a street grid laid out over a painstakingly accurate representation of the city's geography. The IRT map differed from standard maps only in having a few extra lines drawn in showing the transit routes—and, curiously, in laying out Manhattan horizontally. The earliest BRT maps, by contrast, took the opposite approach, portraying New York in a simple, free-form drawing, with no grid and almost no landmarks, solely as a backdrop for the BRT's routes. Subway map designers have spent the better part of a century trying to strike a balance between these two approaches, which attempt to answer two related, but different, questions: where is my geographic destination, and where is my subway stop?

During the 1930s, the individual systems continued to produce their own maps, leaving it to such companies as Geographia and Hagstrom to create all-encompassing versions. In 1938, the Independent line published a station guide showing the IND routes laid out against a simple outline of the boroughs. In keeping with the Machine Age style of its platform walls, with their long, straight lines of color-coded ceramics, the IND mapped its routes as a schematic of solid, brightly colored angular lines with a blocky, Art Deco look.

Unification in 1940 theoretically resulted in unified subway maps, but as late as 1948 the Board of Transportation was publishing separate guides showing all three systems, but using bold-faced lines to

SOUVENIR SCARF *(left and above)*
"Map of New York City's Subway & Elevated Systems"
Circa 1939
Gift of Jill Chase
The centerpiece of this unusual silk scarf is a map showing the IRT, BMT, and Eighth Avenue IND routes, as well as the elevated lines. The scarf dates from around the time of the 1939 World's Fair, one of several New York landmarks shown on the map.

1909 MAP *(overleaf)*
"Routes of the Interborough Rapid Transit Company"
This early IRT map shows the routes of the company's Manhattan, Bronx, and Brooklyn subways in red, and the Manhattan and Bronx elevated lines in blue, all laid out over a detailed rendering of the city's street grid. Like most early IRT maps, it has a horizontal orientation, showing Manhattan from south (left) to north (right).

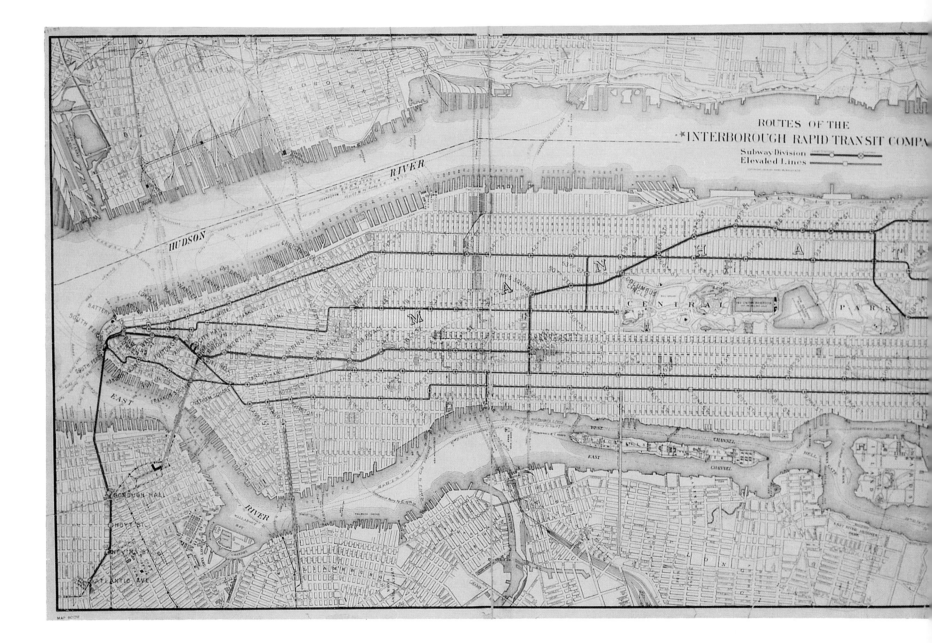

ROUTES OF THE
*INTERBOROUGH RAPID TRANSIT COMPA

Subway Division
Elevated Lines

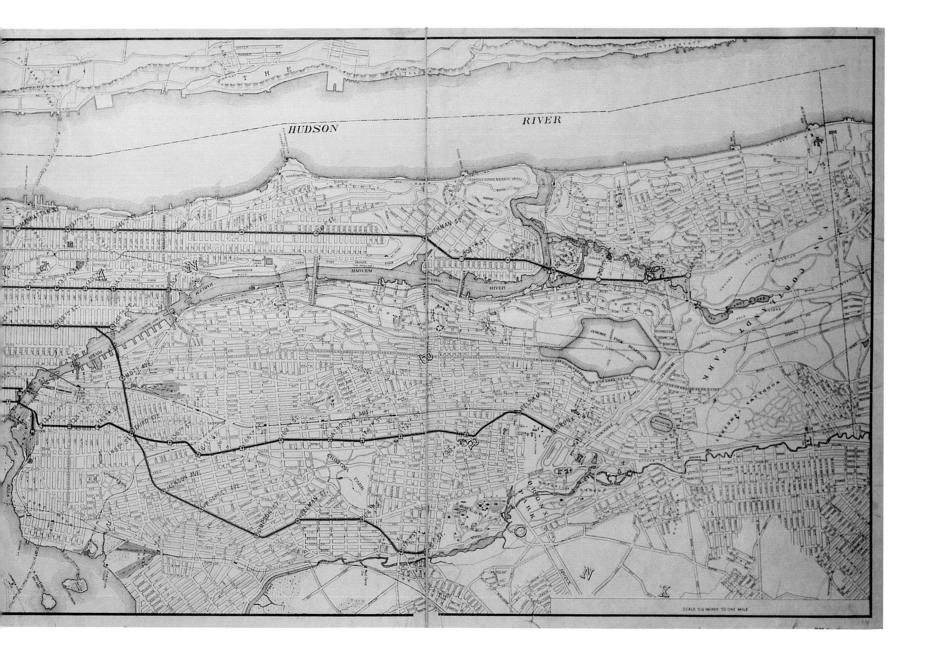

HUDSON RIVER

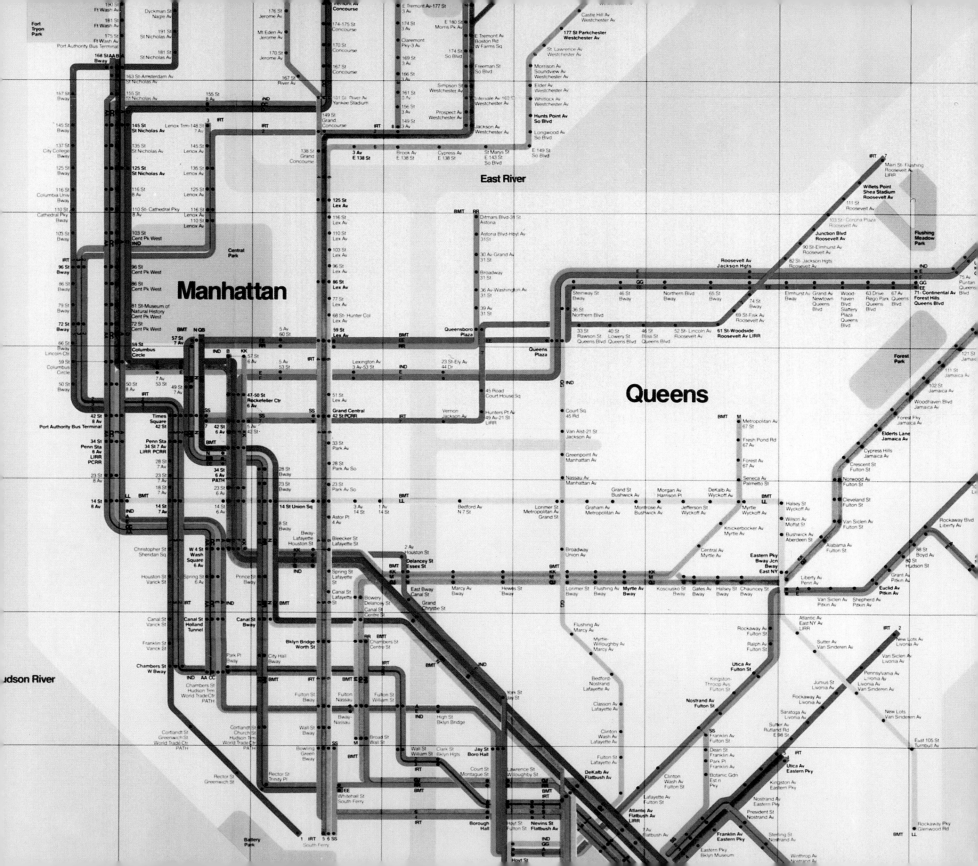

emphasize the IRT routes on the IRT map, and the BMT and IND routes on their respective versions. Finally, in 1958, the recently consolidated Transit Authority commissioned a complete system map from graphic designer George Salomon as part of his system-wide graphics proposal. Salomon produced the first map that could compete, for schematic clarity and attractiveness, with Henry Beck's 1930s trendsetting map of the London Underground, still in use in the British capital. On Salomon's map, the city's boroughs and waterways exist solely as curving abstract blocks of background color. His sharp route lines, solid colors, and sense of orderliness have less to do with the history of map-making than with the history of painting—this was the perfect map for late 1950s avant-garde New York, whose fashionable galleries were displaying the hard-edged styles of Frank Stella and Ellsworth Kelly.

In 1972, the newly-organized MTA brought in Massimo Vignelli, who recast Salomon's map in early 1970s minimalism. Vignelli created a high-style graphic masterpiece, which, unfortunately, severed any remaining connection between the subway lines and the city's geography. His map is by far the most striking of them all, but it is also the least practical. Vignelli reimagined New York and its subway as a series of forty-five- and ninety-degree angles. He gave each subway line its own bright color—fully twenty-two separate colored lines snake around each other in Midtown—set against a stark white background. The result resembles nothing so much as a color-coded circuit board. Design critics loved the map; more practical-minded critics pointed out that besides being hard to read, the map privileged elegance over accuracy even in the relationship of subway

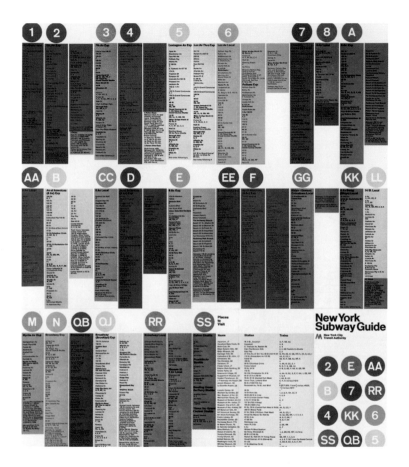

1972 MAP *(front and back)*
"The Metropolitan Transportation Authority Revised Map of Rapid Transit Facilities of New York City Transit Authority" aka "New York Subway Guide"
Designed by Massimo Vignelli
Simple, elegant, and abstract, the Vignelli subway map has long been considered a landmark in modern graphic design. Its very abstraction, however, made the map difficult to understand and generally unpopular.

1919 MAP

"Municipal Railway-Broadway Line Through the Heart of Manhattan"
Printed by Sweeney Lithograph Company
This stylized schematic map of the Broadway route of the New York Municipal Railway—the BRT's subsidiary for subway operations—shows Manhattan laid out horizontally, just like the IRT maps do, but, unlike those, it omits the city's street grid.

1924 MAP

"Routes of the Interborough Rapid Transit Company"
When the IRT began posting maps in its subway cars around 1915, the company used a more abstract, stylized three-color version, shortening and widening Manhattan for convenience and eliminating the detailed street grid of earlier versions. The new map highlighted major parks (in green), rail terminals, museums, cultural attractions, and the three major-league baseball stadiums, in addition to the (red) subway and (blue) elevated lines.

stops. For instance, it positioned the Seventh Avenue line's 50th Street stop *west* of the Eighth Avenue stop. Perhaps unwittingly, Edie Lee Cohen of *Interior Design* underscored the designer's agenda when she wrote in 1980, "A subway map that is geometrically and graphically elegant may give up a few points of readability in exchange for its visual impact." Chief Engineer Parsons would have fired Vignelli on the spot.

Besides embracing the minimalist aesthetic, Vignelli's map was emblematic of New York's 1970s retreat from urban life. As the decade neared its end, New York began to experience a revival linked to a national "back to the cities" movement, a movement led by people who liked to think of cities as more than schematic diagrams. John Tauranac of the MTA, working with Michael Hertz Associates—and, in a first, incorporating straphanger critiques—created a new design that put New York City back into the subway map. The boroughs returned to their natural configurations and began to look more like their old selves. The subway system had grown too complex to be readable if superimposed over the complete city street grid, but there was certainly room to include major streets and avenues, as well as important landmarks. Remarkably, even though the new map contained much more information than its predecessor, it proved easier to read and understand.

The Tauranac / Hertz map has been updated, but essentially it forms the basis for today's version, released in 1998 as "The Map." Taking advantage of newly available computer-assisted design technology, it incorporates yet more information while remaining legible and attractive. For the first time, the subway system map links the subway to the MTA's entire regional network, including buses, commuter railroads, bridges, tunnels, and even the Staten Island Railway, making this the first version to include the whole of Staten Island. Moreover, the Map has become part of a new system of Passenger Information Centers—a combination of neighborhood map, bus map, subway map, guide-a-ride maps, institutional directory, and notice board. Today, if New Yorkers or visitors occasionally take the wrong train, it's their own fault.

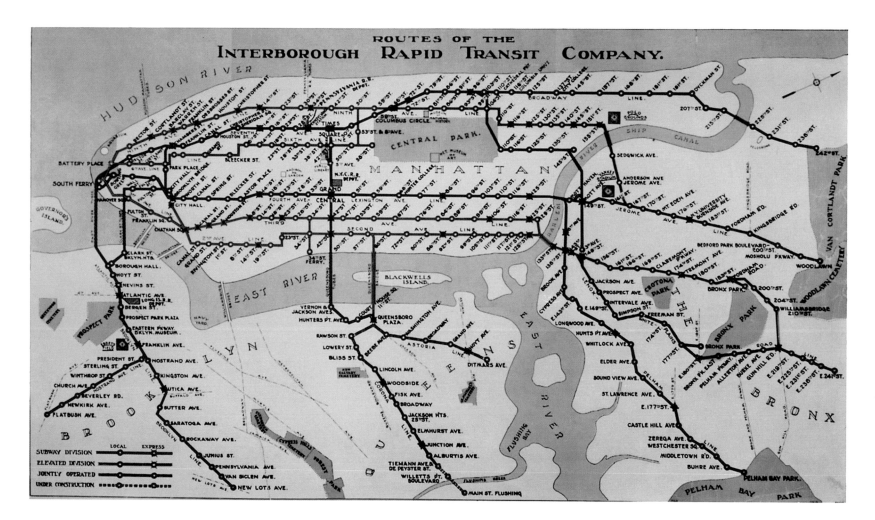

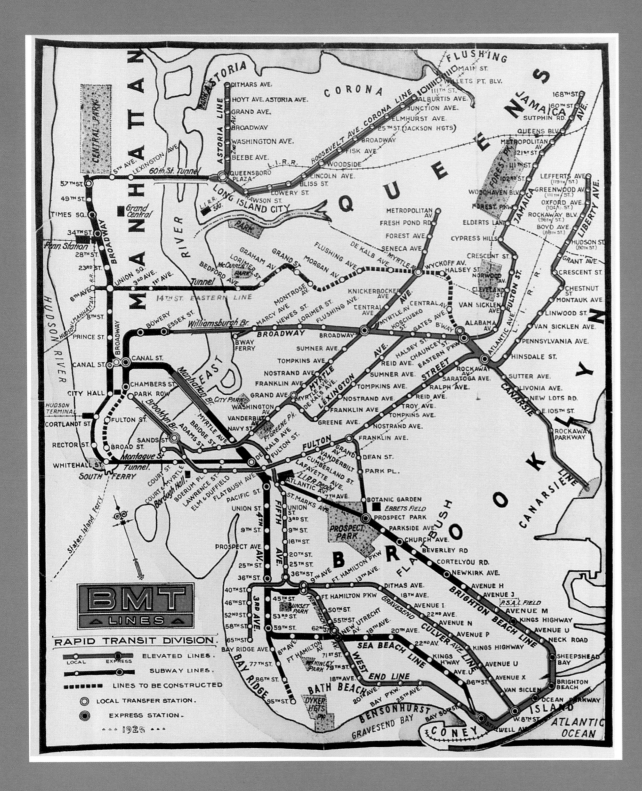

1925 MAP
"BMT Lines Rapid Transit Division"
Using the more customary vertical format for Manhattan, the BMT adopted a clear, simplified, geographically-based map style. The map shows routes as thick, exaggerated lines—with elevated sections (in red) distinguished from subways (black)—and highlights the East River bridges and tunnels.

CIRCA 1935 MAP
"Transportation Map of New York (Subway and Elevated Systems)"
Made by Geographia Map Company, New York
The individual systems produced maps showing only their own routes, leaving it to commercial map companies to create maps showing the entire subway. Geographia's map indicated the individual systems—IRT, BMT, and IND, as well as the Hudson and Manhattan Tubes (today's PATH system)—with separate colors (red, blue, green, and black), superimposed over a generic regional map that included major streets and avenues.

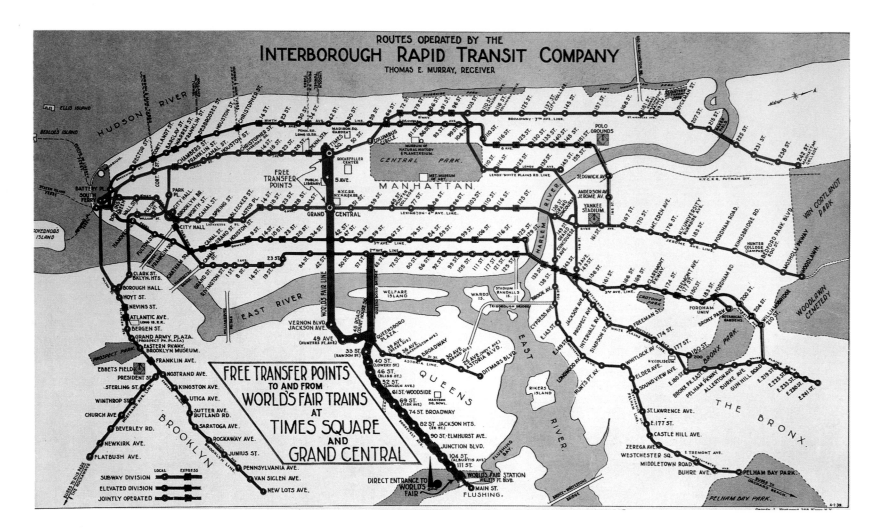

1939 MAP

"Routes Operated by the Interborough Rapid Transit Company, Thomas E. Murray, Receiver"
April 1, 1939
Printed by George J. Nostrand
To promote subway travel to the 1939 World's Fair, the IRT produced a map highlighting routes to the fairgrounds and special "free transfer points." This map was one of the last produced by the bankrupt but still independent company just before unification of the city subway system.

1938 MAP

"Station Guide, Independent City Owned Rapid Transit Railroad"
In keeping with the Machine Age aesthetic of Vickers's color-coded ceramic walls, the schematic, almost abstract, IND map uses solid, angular lines over cloud-like silhouettes of the boroughs. Each of the system's lines is represented by a specific color. The New York Transit Museum currently occupies the Court Street stop on the HH local.

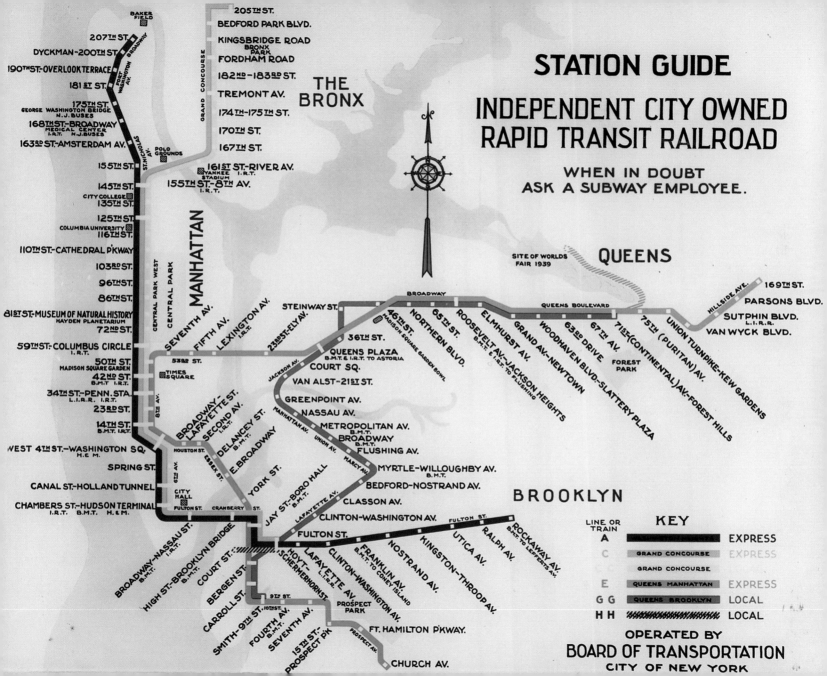

STATION GUIDE

INDEPENDENT CITY OWNED RAPID TRANSIT RAILROAD

WHEN IN DOUBT ASK A SUBWAY EMPLOYEE.

THE BRONX

QUEENS

MANHATTAN

BROOKLYN

SITE OF WORLDS FAIR 1939

KEY

LINE OR TRAIN				
A				EXPRESS
C	GRAND CONCOURSE			EXPRESS
CC	GRAND CONCOURSE			
E	QUEENS MANHATTAN			EXPRESS
GG	QUEENS BROOKLYN			LOCAL
HH				LOCAL

OPERATED BY
BOARD OF TRANSPORTATION
CITY OF NEW YORK

Stations (Bronx / upper Manhattan):
BAKER FIELD
207TH ST.
DYCKMAN–200TH ST.
190TH ST.–OVERLOOK TERRACE
181ST ST.
175TH ST. GEORGE WASHINGTON BRIDGE N.J. BUSES
168TH ST.–BROADWAY MEDICAL CENTER I.R.T. N.J. BUSES
163RD ST.–AMSTERDAM AV.
155TH ST.
145TH ST.
135TH ST. CITY COLLEGE
125TH ST.
116TH ST. COLUMBIA UNIVERSITY
110TH ST.–CATHEDRAL P'KWAY
103RD ST.
96TH ST.
86TH ST.
81ST ST.–MUSEUM OF NATURAL HISTORY HAYDEN PLANETARIUM
72ND ST.
59TH ST.–COLUMBUS CIRCLE I.R.T.
50TH ST. MADISON SQUARE GARDEN
42ND ST.
34TH ST.–PENN. STA. L.I.R.R. I.R.T.
23RD ST.
14TH ST. B.M.T. I.R.T.
WEST 4TH ST.–WASHINGTON SQ. H. & M.
SPRING ST.
CANAL ST.–HOLLAND TUNNEL
CHAMBERS ST.–HUDSON TERMINAL I.R.T. B.M.T. H. & M.

Grand Concourse line:
205TH ST.
BEDFORD PARK BLVD.
KINGSBRIDGE ROAD BRONX PARK
FORDHAM ROAD
182ND–183RD ST.
TREMONT AV.
174TH–175TH ST.
170TH ST.
167TH ST.
161ST ST.–RIVER AV. YANKEE STADIUM I.R.T.
155TH ST.–8TH AV. I.R.T.
POLO GROUNDS
ST. NICHOLAS AV.
FORT WASHINGTON AV.

Manhattan / Queens labels:
BROADWAY
CENTRAL PARK WEST
CENTRAL PARK
SEVENTH AV.
FIFTH AV.
LEXINGTON AV. I.R.T.
8TH AV.
53RD ST.
TIMES SQUARE
23RD ST.–ELY AV.
STEINWAY ST.
36TH ST.
46TH ST. MADISON SQUARE GARDEN BOWL
NORTHERN BLVD.
65TH ST.
ROOSEVELT AV.–JACKSON HEIGHTS B.M.T. & I.R.T. TO FLUSHING
ELMHURST AV.
GRAND AV.–NEWTOWN
WOODHAVEN BLVD.–SLATTERY PLAZA
63RD DRIVE
67TH AV.
71ST (CONTINENTAL) AV.–FOREST HILLS
75TH (PURITAN) AV.
FOREST PARK
UNION TURNPIKE–KEW GARDENS
QUEENS BOULEVARD
HILLSIDE AV.
169TH ST.
PARSONS BLVD.
SUTPHIN BLVD.
VAN WYCK BLVD. L.I.R.R.

Queens Plaza area:
QUEENS PLAZA B.M.T. & I.R.T. TO ASTORIA
COURT SQ.
VAN ALST–21ST ST.
GREENPOINT AV.
NASSAU AV.
METROPOLITAN AV. B.M.T.
BROADWAY B.M.T.
FLUSHING AV.
MYRTLE–WILLOUGHBY AV. B.M.T.
BEDFORD–NOSTRAND AV.
CLASSON AV.
CLINTON–WASHINGTON AV.
FULTON ST.
JACKSON AV.
UNION AV.
MANHATTAN AV.
MARCY AV.

Lower Manhattan / Brooklyn:
BROADWAY–LAFAYETTE ST.
SECOND AV.
DELANCEY ST. B.M.T.
E. BROADWAY
YORK ST.
JAY ST.–BORO HALL B.M.T.
HOUSTON ST.
6TH AV.
ESSEX ST.
CITY HALL
FULTON ST.
CRANBERRY ST.
LAFAYETTE AV.
BROADWAY–NASSAU ST. I.R.T.
HIGH ST.–BROOKLYN BRIDGE B.M.T.
COURT ST.
BERGEN ST.
CARROLL ST.
SMITH–9TH ST.
9TH ST.
FOURTH AV. B.M.T.
SEVENTH AV.
15TH ST.–PROSPECT PK.
CHURCH AV.
FT. HAMILTON P'KWAY.
PROSPECT PARK
HOYT–SCHERMERHORN ST.
LAFAYETTE AV. L.I.R.R.
CLINTON–WASHINGTON AV.
FRANKLIN AV. B.M.T. TO CONEY ISLAND
NOSTRAND AV.
KINGSTON–THROOP AV.
UTICA AV.
RALPH AV.
ROCKAWAY AV. B.M.T. TO LEFFERTS AV.
FULTON ST.
10TH ST.

Station Guide New York City Transit System

Owned by the City of New York
and
Operated by the Board of Transportation

LEGEND

▬▬▬	IND LINES	⊙	EXPRESS STOPS
▬▬▬	IRT LINES	⊸	LOCAL STOPS
▬▬▬	BMT LINES		ELEVATED LINES
		1471	HOUSE NUMBERS

Note: For legibility, all Streets and St. have been omitted.
Example: 42nd Street Station shown as 42 only.

Copyright by HAGSTROM COMPANY, INC., N.Y., Map Makers
311 Broadway, New York 7, N.Y.

Service Information IND Division

MARKER	TRAIN	TERMINALS	ROUTE
A	Washington Heights Exp.	207th St. and Euclid Ave. *(Local in Brooklyn at non-rush hours)*	8th AVE.
AA	Washington Heights Local	168th St. and Hudson Terminal *(Non-rush hours only)*	8th AVE.
BB	Washington Heights Local	168th St. and 34th St. at 6th Ave. *(Rush hours only)*	6th AVE.
CC	Bronx Concourse Local	Bedf'd Park and B'way—Lafayette St. *(Rush hours only)*	8th AVE.
D	Bronx Concourse Express	205th St. and Hudson Terminal	6th AVE.
E	Queens-Manhattan Exp.	179th St. (Jam'd) and B'way L'f'yette St. *(Rush hours to B'way, East New York via Fulton St. Tunnel)*	8th AVE.
F	Queens-Manhattan Exp.	179th St. (Jamaica) and Church Ave.	6th AVE. HOUSTON ST.
GG	Queens-Brooklyn Local	Continental Ave.—Forest Hills and Smith—9th Sts.	BROOKLYN CROSSTOWN

Service Information IRT Division

TRAIN	TERMINALS
Lex. Ave.-Jerome Ave. Exp.	Woodlawn Road, Atlantic Ave. and South Ferry—Utica Ave.
Lex. Ave.-White Plains Rd. Exp.	E. 241st St. and Utica Ave. *(Does not operate 12:04 a.m. to 5:16 a.m.)*
B'way-7th Ave. Express	242nd St.—Van Cortlandt Park and New Lots Ave.—Flatbush Ave.
7th Ave. Local	145th St.—Lenox Ave. and South Ferry *(from 12:04 a.m. to 5:16 a.m. to East 241st St.)*
B'way-7th Ave. Local	137th St.—Broadway and South Ferry *(Does not operate 12:04 a.m. to 5:36 a.m.)*
Lexington Ave. Local	Pelham Bay Park and Brooklyn Bridge *(During rush hours alternate trains Exp. on Pelham Line)*
Flushing Line (Local & Exp.)	Times Square and Main St.
Dyre Avenue Line	East 180th St. and Dyre Ave.
42nd Street Shuttle	Times Square and Grand Central
Bowling Green Shuttle	Bowling Green and South Ferry
155th St. to 167th St. Shuttle	155th St.—8th Ave. and 167th St.—Jerome Ave.
3rd Avenue Line	Gunhill Road and Chatham Square

Service Information BMT Division

TRAIN	TERMINALS	ROUTE
Brighton Beach Express	57th St.—Times Square and Brighton Beach	VIA BRIDGE
Brighton Beach Local	57th St.—Astoria and Coney Island	VIA TUNNEL
Culver-Nassau	Coney Island and Chambers St.	VIA TUNNEL
Sea Beach Express	Times Square and Coney Island	VIA BRIDGE
West End Express	Times Square and Coney Island	VIA BRIDGE
West End Short Line	Chambers St. and 62nd St. (B'klyn) *(Rush hours only)*	VIA NASSAU ST. LOOP
4th Avenue Local	Astoria and 95th St.—Fort Hamilton	VIA TUNNEL
14th Street—Canarsie	8th Ave. (Man.) and Canarsie (Rockaway Parkway)	
14th St.—Fulton St.	8th Ave. (Man.) and Lefferts Ave. *(Rush hours only)*	
Franklin Ave. Shuttle	Franklin Ave. and Prospect Park	
Fulton St. Line	Rockaway Ave.—Eastern Parkway and Lefferts Ave.	
Myrtle Ave. Line	Metropolitan Ave. and Bridge Jay Sts.	
Myrtle-Chambers Line	Metropolitan Ave. and Chambers St.	VIA BROADWAY, BROOKLYN
Jamaica Line	168th St. and Broad St.	VIA BROADWAY, BROOKLYN
Broadway Short Line	Canal St. and Atlantic Ave.	VIA BROADWAY, BROOKLYN

Lost Property Office

73 Rockwell Place (near Fulton Street), Brooklyn 17, N.Y.
Telephone: MAin 5-6200
9:00 A.M. to 4:00 P.M. Daily, Closed Sundays & Holidays

BOARD OF TRANSPORTATION
OF THE CITY OF NEW YORK
GENERAL OFFICES
370 JAY ST., BROOKLYN 1, N.Y.
Telephone ULster 2-5000

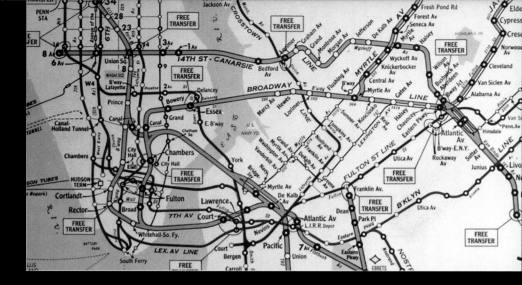

1948 MAP

"Station Guide, New York City Transit System"
Board of Transportation of the City of New York
In 1948, the Board of Transportation adapted a
Hagstrom Company city map to serve as the
basis for a series of four nearly identical guides
to the subway and elevated system. Though all
the guides showed the same routes and
stations—indicating the IRT in blue, the BMT
in yellow, and the IND in red—each subway
division had a version emphasizing its own
routes with thicker lines. The fourth map
represented all routes equally.

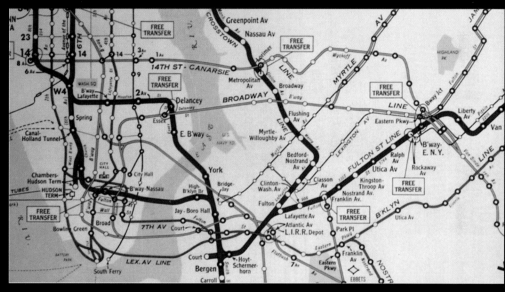

MAP DETAILS

"Station Guide, BMT, IND, and IRT Divisions,
New York City Transit System"
1948
Board of Transportation of the City of New York

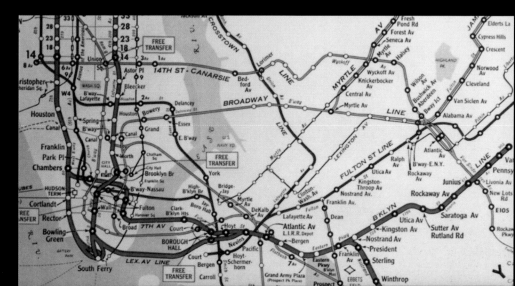

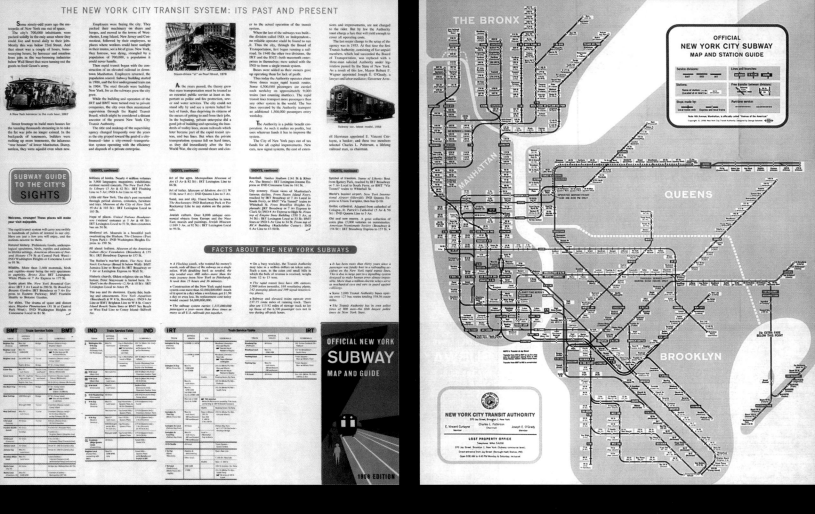

1958 MAP

"Official New York Subway Map and Guide"

Designed by George Salomon

Salomon's map for the Transit Authority—the first to show the entire system—gives the three once-separate systems equal weight and color (red, IRT; green, BMT; black, IND). Though abstract and stylized—representing the boroughs as a series of simplified gray masses— Salomon's map still bears enough similarity to the city's geography to be readily usable.

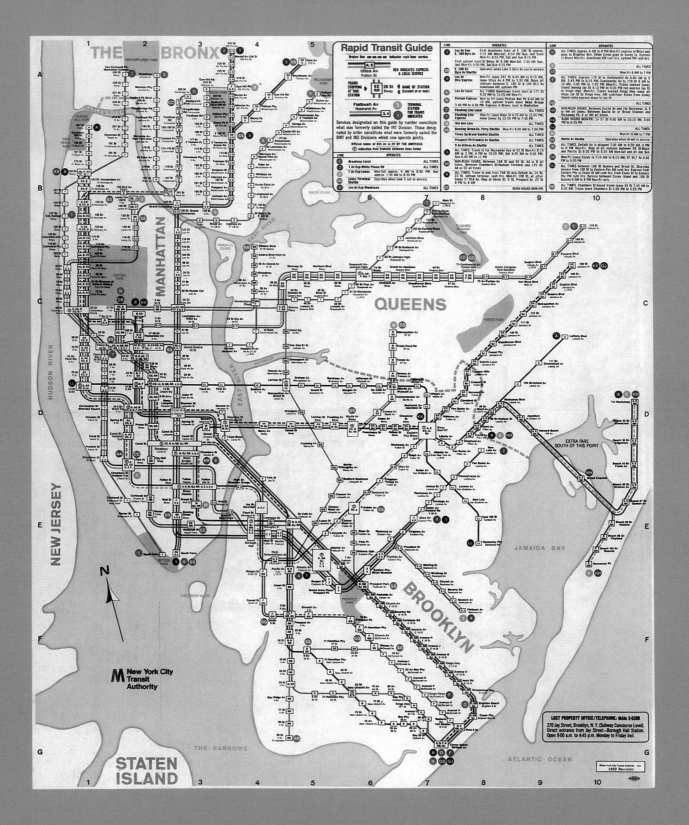

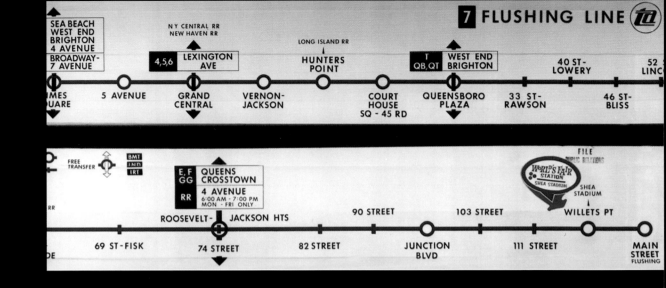

1969 MAP (FIRST ISSUED 1967)
"New York City Rapid Transit Map and Station Guide"
While earlier maps, including Salomon's, designated each subway division (IRT, BMT, IND) with a single color, the Transit Authority introduced a new system in 1967 that assigned a separate color to each route (with some duplication) along with a number or letter. The new map kept much of Salomon's stylized design, but added major parks to help make the abstract borough representations a little more realistic. This 1969 version of the map sports the new MTA logo.

SUBWAY STRIP MAP
"7 Flushing Line"
Circa 1964
One of the few subway lines to have its own dedicated fleet—the same cars always running on the same route—the number 7 Flushing line also had its own single-route horizontal strip map, designed for the 1964–1965 World's Fair and the opening of the new Shea Stadium. The strip map adapted the style of Salomon's design, with modified colors.

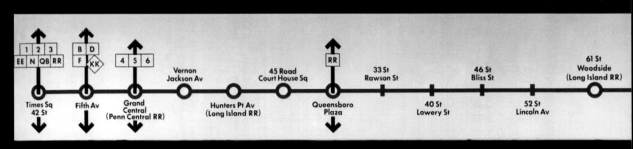

SUBWAY STRIP MAP
"7" Line
1972
An early 1970s revision brought the Flushing line strip map into conformity with the Unimark color and graphics program

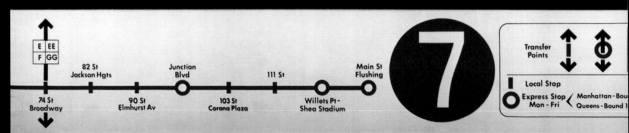

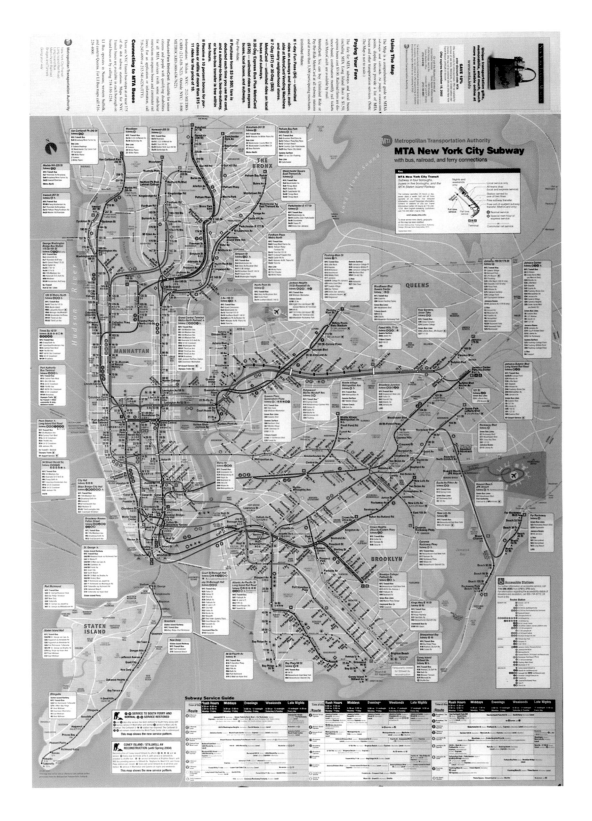

DETAIL

MTA New York City Transit Map
1979

"THE MAP"

"Metropolitan Transportation Authority
New York Subway with bus, railroad,
and ferry connections"
1998 (September 2002 edition)
Designed by Michael Hertz Associates

ADVERTISING

Board the subway, look around, and you could find yourself longing to join alluring models as they sip expensive scotch. Or nodding to the rhythmic cadences of poetry old and new. Or absorbing the subway's version of the American Dream: mastering English, winning huge cash settlements, and clearing up your skin with a chemical fruit peel.

Welcome to the world of subway advertising. With a captive audience of millions of riders every day, the subway is a promoter's dream, the place where mass transit meets mass marketing. Ads are everywhere in American culture, but they have an aesthetic all their own in the subway—an aesthetic drawn on the one hand from the system's physical characteristics

ADVERTISING IN IRT STATION
Circa 1904

ADVERTISING IN CITY HALL IRT STATION
Circa 1920

and on the other from its peculiar mix of the quirky, the slick, and the highbrow, its odd combination of commercialized temptation, self-help, and earnest public service.

The early planners of the subway imagined it pristine and commercial free. In 1894, Chief Engineer Parsons lambasted London's Underground for "the hideous advertising signs" on its station walls. The first IRT contract seemed to prohibit ads in the subway, and Heins & LaFarge's designs made no allowance for them. No sooner had the system opened, however, than framed posters began appearing on station walls and even railings—ads for Baker's Cocoa, Evans Ale, and "A Positive Cure for Constipation" hanging over the carefully designed walls, from nails driven into the tiles. Protest came quickly and loudly. "Cheap and nasty," declared Rapid Transit Commissioner Charles Stewart Smith. "We do not believe," harrumphed the Architectural League, "in advertising signs jammed against works of art." John DeWitt Warner, chairman of the Municipal Art Commission, hoped that the posters would be "smashed by gentlemen" who would "kick or crush them in abatement of a nuisance."

The Manhattan borough president ordered the advertisements removed. The IRT's August Belmont, however, had read his contract carefully and found that it excluded only those advertisements "which shall interfere with easy identification of stations." The parties went to court, and Belmont won. In the mid-1920s, as Squire J. Vickers planned the new IND stations—city-owned and operated, unlike Belmont's IRT—several designers argued against permitting ads. But now the income would accrue to the city, rather than to a

private contractor. "We therefore," wrote Vickers, "made provision in the wall surfaces at both mezzanine and platform levels for advertising signs of standard size. . . . It is hoped that the revenue will prove to be an efficient 'balm for hurt minds.'"

Subway station wall posters differ little from wall posters anywhere; it's the so-called "car cards" in the trains that have a more distinctive subway style. These now appear in one of two formats: the traditional jumble inherited from nineteenth-century streetcars and elevated trains—dozens of cards lined up cheek by jowl in no particular order, a cardboard reflection of the diversity of passengers jammed together on the seats—and the new single-car campaigns, an entire subway car devoted to one message.

Car cards advertising national brands bring the style and language of Madison Avenue to the subway. By contrast, the come-ons from extension schools and laser-vision clinics seem hopelessly amateurish—odd photography, curious grammar. Yet those are often the most memorable ads, perhaps because of their very quirkiness. Whether homegrown or high-priced, both types of ads share the subway experience; each message reduced to a uniform cardboard rectangle lined up in the horizontal band just above the windows and doors, or, more prominently, a larger rectangle in a series of spaces shared with the subway map.

At various times, the subway has tried to encourage more stylish ads. In the late 1940s, the New York Subways Advertising Company mounted a campaign of sample designs that went out in the mail, up on the station walls, and into the cars. With titles like "23

Minutes with your Customer" or "Selling . . . Selling . . . Selling . . . SOLD," the cards highlighted the value of professional design—of color, repetition, and other tricks of the advertising trade. Today's single-car approach represents the most recent effort to promote visual order—virtually guaranteeing a sophisticated campaign, and creating a unified, car-long look emphasizing the sleek lines of the latest subway cars.

Public service ads today range from glossy and sophisticated educational campaigns on domestic violence, to the Poetry in Motion series sponsored by the Poetry Society of America, to "SubTalk" service announcements, to Arts for Transit posters. During the 1990s, "Decision," a bilingual AIDS education cartoon serial drama, unexpectedly became a cult classic followed avidly by New Yorkers. All these cards descend from homier predecessors like the "Meet Miss Subways" series, which between 1941 and 1977 celebrated hundreds of New York women in car cards with photos and bios. Or *The Subway Sun*, its title set in Gothic type to mimic a newspaper's front page, which began in the late teens as a format for the IRT's public announcements and reached its zenith after World War II under the able pen of cartoonist Amelia Opdyke Jones. "Oppy" created hundreds of caricatures of ill-mannered subway behavior that today's New Yorkers would instantly recognize, with snappy titles, like "Lady! PUL-EAZE" for a woman jamming her packages and umbrella into her neighbors.

Subway ads cheap and nasty? Sometimes. But a nuisance? Never. Without them, what would straphangers do for entertainment?

SUBWAY POSTER

June 1942

Designed and produced by New York City WPA War Services
During World War II, the Board of Transportation posted public service notices designed by artists employed by the federal Works Progress Administration. Many of these posters—often produced in collaboration with other city departments and agencies—promoted home-front preparedness, conservation, safety, patriotism, and free recreation and entertainment, especially use of city parks' facilities and beaches. Simple, striking, and elegant, this two-color poster promoted fitness "for defense," city pools, and use of the New York City transit system.

Amelia Opdyke Jones, a protégée of Fred G. Cooper who signed her work "Oppy," took over inking the *The Subway Sun* from Cooper in 1946 and continued to design them for the next twenty years. It is said that Oppy first introduced the term "litterbug" through the *Sun*.

ORIGINAL ART

For *The Subway Sun*, Vol. XIV, No. 19
1947

For *The Subway Sun,* Vol. XV, No. 3
1948

In the early 1960s, departing from the tradition of single-frame pictures, Oppy designed several multipanel cartoons for *The Subway Sun*.

SUBWAY CAR POSTERS

The Subway Sun, Vol. XXV, No. 33
1961
Produced by the New York City Transit Authority

The Subway Sun, Vol. XXV, No. 34
1961
Produced by the New York City Transit Authority

SUBWAY CAR CARDS

The Subway Sun, Vol. XVII, No. 12
August 1950
Produced by the Board of Transportation

The Subway Sun, Vol. XVII, No. 9
1950
Produced by New York City Transit Authority

SUBWAY CAR POSTER

The Subway Sun, Vol. XIII, No. 4
February 21, 1946
Produced by the Board of Transportation
Prior to 1948, all *Subway Sun* posters, like
most subway system notices, were printed on
thin paper, generally fifteen by twenty inches,
and pasted on the inside of car windows.

SUBWAY CAR POSTER
The Subway Sun, Vol. XXIII, No. 13
Circa 1956
Produced by New York City Transit Authority
This nighttime photograph of the 207th Street Yard after a light
snowfall dramatizes one of the themes of later *Subway Sun*
posters—the skills and contributions of subway workers.

ORIGINAL ART

For *The Subway Sun,* Vol. XVII, No. 10
August 1950

For *The Subway Sun,* Vol. XVIII, No. 7
August 1951

For *The Subway Sun,* Vol. XVII, No. 15
November 1950
Designed and painted by Oppy (Amelia Opdyke Jones)

HUNGER ON WHEELS

Showing foods and drinks to millions of
hungry and thirsty homeward bound
New Yorkers daily, just when they want them
most... this is Subway Advertising.

FROM CAR TO COUNTER

IS A MATTER OF MOMENTS

FRED CHANCE

...in sight...in light

...all day...all night

SUBWAY CARCARDS

Selections from
THIS IS SUBWAY ADVERTISING
Circa 1946
Produced by New York Subways Advertising Company, Inc.
In 1946, the New York Subways Advertising Company invited
some of the nation's most prominent graphic artists to
create car cards promoting subway advertising. The company
published two dozen of these designs as a portfolio of
miniatures—half-sized copies of standard eleven-by-twenty-
one-inch subway car cards. Each card also featured, on
the flip side, a biography of the artist and an explanation
of the poster's advertising techniques. "As we had hoped,"
NYSA declared in the introduction to the portfolio,
"these artists have given a demonstration of the almost
unlimited possibilities of the medium. The obvious
effectiveness of their designs may well encourage advertisers
and their agencies to entrust their car card designs and
copy to the most capable hands available."

NO. 3
Designed by E. McKnight Kauffer, New York, New York
Kauffer—a leader in poster design, and especially known for
his work for the London Underground—took an almost
surreal approach to this assignment.

NO. 12
Designed by Fred Chance, New York, New York
Chance, known for his magazine covers, produced a concise
and abstract, even dreamlike, design.

NO. 13
Designed by Sascha Maurer, New York, New York

NO. 21

Designed by Erik Nitsche, New York, New York

In this particularly clever reference to the subway, the iris and pupil of an (unusually receptive) eye are one with the tracks, platforms, and tunnel of a subway station filled with people. Typically for International Style graphics, the imagery is simple and the forms and typeface are streamlined.

NO. 18

Designed by Wulf Stapelfeldt, Norwalk, Connecticut

Stapelfeldt's sample car card poses the question so critical to product advertising: "How do people get to know a name?" Using a soft-cartoon style with subtle color shading, he offers the answer: "Repetition, repetition, repetition, repetition, repetition . . ."

NO. 25

Designed by Fred G. Cooper, New York, New York
Cooper—already a well-known cartoonist and illustrator—designed many of the IRT's *Subway Sun* cards in the late 1920s and 1930s. He set the tone and style that his protégée, Oppy, would adopt in the late 1940s.

NO. 2

Designed by Trude Margo, New York, New York
Cosmetics and fashion advertising artist Margo applied her "elegant and sophisticated" approach—soft lines and pastel colors—to subway car card design.

NO. 11

Designed by Robert Osborn, New York, New York
Bright colors, cartoon figures, punning text, and tight design characterize Osborn's approach to showing evening rush-hour trains with their captive audience of "people almost drooling with thoughts of dinner."

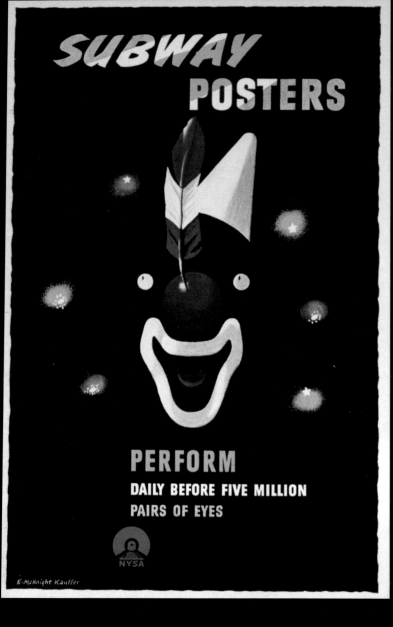

Selections from

SERIES OF NEW YORK SUBWAY POSTER DESIGNS

Circa 1948

Produced by New York Subways Advertising Company, Inc.
In 1947 and 1948—as a sequel to the This Is Subway
Advertising car card portfolio—the New York Subways
Advertising Company created a mailing campaign using a
dozen miniature subway poster designs created, like their
predecessors, by leading American artists. The campaign won
the Direct Mail Advertising Association's top award. The
posters promoted the advantages of subway advertising:
"COLOR—all you want; REPETITION—26 times a month;
COVERAGE—9 out of 10 New York City adults are subway riders.

NO. 1

Designed by E. McKnight Kauffer, New York, New York

NO. 4

Designed by Jean Carlu, New York, New York
A leading French modernist designer, Carlu came to the
United States in 1940.

NO. 5

Designed by Otis Shepard, Chicago, Illinois

SUBWAY CAR POSTER

1964
Produced by the New York City Transit Authority,
in cooperation with the New York World's Fair
1964–1965 Corporation
Printed in the World's Fair's official colors, blue
and orange, this poster includes a cartoon
illustration of the new R-36 and R-33S subway
cars and the fair's Unisphere logo.

In the late 1950s, Oppy's designs for *The*
Subway Sun became bolder, using more than
one color and tending to brighter hues.

SUBWAY CAR CARDS

The Subway Sun, Vol. XXV, No. 9
1958
Produced by New York City Transit Authority

The Subway Sun, Vol. XXV, No. 16
1958
Produced by New York City Transit Authority

SUBWAY CAR CARD

Circa 1961

Produced by the New York City Transit Authority

In an early 1960s campaign promoting subway courtesy, the Transit Authority produced a series of "Mr. Zookeeper" contest car cards in the spirit, if not the style, of Oppy's *Subway Sun* etiquette cartoons. The subway car in this illustration actually includes two sketches of Oppy car cards current at the time—"Please, Sorry, Thanks" and "Be a Knight for a Day." The passenger who proposed the most appropriate name for the discourteous subway elephant won 500 tokens (a year's supply).

SUBWAY POSTER

Circa 1970

Designed by Springer-Leon

In 1970, the Transit Authority held a public service exhibit of employee art in the mezzanine of the 57th Street IND Station—then among the city's newest, having opened July 1, 1968. The stylized design of this promotional poster includes a rendering of the station's International Style entrance.

Cast your postcard vote today - pick the next two ※MISS SUBWAYS

RUTH ZALDUONDO	HARRIETTE SCHWARTZ	LINDA LANNA	CAROL BROWN	ALICE JONES	DIANE WEISGERBER
Secretary, Radio Station WHN	Reporter, Radio Free Europe	Student, Finch College	Administrative Assistant, MacKay-Shields Financial Corp.	Secretary, Select Magazines, Inc.	Secretary, City Investing Company

Write the names of TWO of these finalists on a postcard (Only ONE postcard per voter allowed)
—sign your name and address and mail before May 7, 1973 to... **N.Y. SUBWAYS ADVERTISING CO., INC.** 750 Third Avenue, New York, N.Y. 10017

PHOTOGRAPHED BY *James J. Kriegsmann*
PHOTOGRAPHER OF CELEBRITIES

"MISS SUBWAYS" is a service mark of NEW YORK SUBWAYS ADVERTISING CO., INC.

※MISS SUBWAYS

CAROL ANN NORMAN	SONIA DOMINGUEZ	STACEY-MARIE MAUPIN	CHARLOTTE SEVERSON	MARCIA KILPATRICK	CHIM YI
Ass't Manager, Tower Health Club	Data Processing, Bache & Co.	Secretary, Paragon Pictures	Sec'y-Artist, Womankind Unlimited	Administrative Ass't, Off Track Betting Corp.	Ass't Art Director Rothchild Printing Co.

Meet *MISS SUBWAYS Ayana Lawson

Ayana's a budding young actress. She's devoted a lot of time to training in drama technique, voice, dance and modeling. Thus far, she's had roles in four off-Broadway plays and in two movies.

To support herself fulltime, Ayana works as head teller at a branch of National Bank of North America. This fall, she plans to take some social work courses at Fordham U.

Ayana likes to cook, ride bikes, dance, roller-skate and paint.

PHOTOGRAPHED BY James J. Kriegsmann PHOTOGRAPHER OF CELEBRITIES

* MISS SUBWAYS is a service mark of NEW YORK SUBWAYS ADVERTISING CO., INC.

SUBWAY CAR CARDS

Ballot Cards for Miss Subways
1973–1974
James J. Kriegsmann, photographer
Produced by New York Subways Advertising Co., Inc.
The Miss Subways contest, held monthly from 1941 to 1977, quickly became a pop-culture phenomenon—and inspired the 1944 movie musical *On the Town* (by Leonard Bernstein, Betty Comden, and Adolph Green), in which three sailors ashore on leave search for "Miss Turnstiles."

SUBWAY CAR CARD

Circa 1970–1975
James J. Kriegsmann, photographer
Produced by New York Subways Advertising Co., Inc.

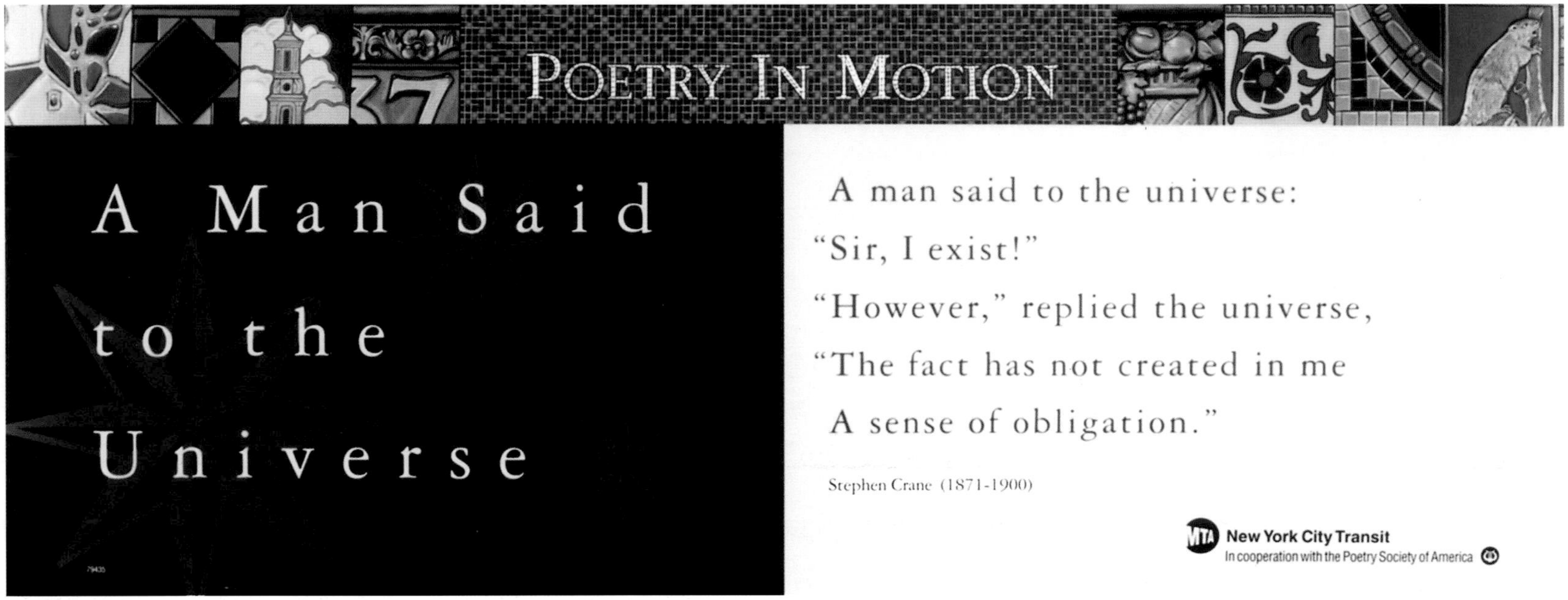

A Man Said to the Universe

A man said to the universe:

"Sir, I exist!"

"However," replied the universe,

"The fact has not created in me

A sense of obligation."

Stephen Crane (1871-1900)

MTA New York City Transit
In cooperation with the Poetry Society of America

"POETRY IN MOTION" SUBWAY CAR CARD
July 1994
Poem by Stephen Crane
Produced by MTA New York City Transit in cooperation with
the Poetry Society of America
In 1992—inspired by a similar program in the London Underground—the
MTA and the Poetry Society of America jointly developed the Poetry in Motion
program, scattering poem car cards among the ads on subways and buses.

"SUBTALK" SUBWAY CAR CARD
Circa 1993
Produced by MTA New York City Transit
A generation after Oppy's *Subway Sun* series, cartoon figures reappeared—
in brighter colors—in SubTalk safety and courtesy car cards.

"SUBTALK" SUBWAY CAR CARD
1992
Produced by MTA New York City Transit
In the early 1990s, the MTA began producing SubTalk car cards with service
announcements. This card does not use images—instead, it catches
the rider's attention with two colors of type and concise, clever wording.

Gonna get you!

**Hold on. Stand away from the sides.
Never sit or play on escalators.**

Escalators can get you.
They catch schoolbags, clothes and
sneakers. They can even catch you.

SubTalk   **Ride Smart**

SubTalk

Queens and R trains now run every 10 minutes during the day on weekends. Do you get the idea we want you to ride the train more?

MTA M The Transit Authority. Going your way.

Service improvements are part of Fare Deal, an MTA plan to give New York the best public transportation.

Attention ❶ ❾ Passengers Going to South Ferry

Please move to one of the first five cars of this train in preparation for arrival at South Ferry. The rear cars will not be opened at South Ferry because the station cannot accommodate the full length of the train. Thank you for your cooperation.

A l'attention des passagers des lignes 1/9 dont la destination est South Ferry
Si votre destination est South Ferry, veuillez vous diriger vers l'un des cinq wagons de tête de ce train. Le quai de cette station étant plus court que le train, les portes des wagons de queue resteront fermées. Nous vous remercions de votre coopération.

Achtung 1/9 passagiere in richtung South Ferry
Begeben Sie sich bitte vor der Ankunft in South Ferry in einen der fünf vorderen Wagen dieses Zuges. Die Türen der hinteren Wagen werden an South Ferry nicht geöffnet, da der Zug zu lang für die Station ist. Wir danken Ihnen für Ihr Verständnis.

Attenzione 1/9 passeggeri diretti a South Ferry
Quando il treno si sta preparando all'arrivo a South Ferry, portarsi all'altezza di una delle prime cinque vetture. Le vetture che si trovano sul retro non entreranno in stazione, perche` la stazione di South Ferry non è in grado di accogliere l'intera lunghezza del treno. Grazie per la vostra collaborazione.

Atencion Pasajeros de los trenes 1/9 que van a la estación South Ferry
Por favor pasen a los primeros cinco vagones de este tren para prepararse para la llegada a la estación South Ferry. Los carros de la parte posterior del tren no abren las puertas en South Ferry porque la estación no puede acomodar el tren en toda su extensión. Gracias por su cooperación.

К сведению пассажиров, следующих до станции South Ferry на поездах № 1 или № 9
Если Вы собираетесь выйти на станции South Ferry, пройдите, пожалуйста, в один из пяти головных вагонов поезда. Двери задних вагонов на станции South Ferry не откроются, так как платформа на станции слишком коротка. Просим прощения за это маленькое неудобство.

乘坐1/9號地車前往南渡口的乘客請注意
地車即將進入南渡口站時，請向前面五節車廂移動預備下車。由於南渡口站不能容納整個車身，地車後面幾節車廂的門在南渡口將不打開。謝謝合作。

| 1 | 2 | 3 | 4 | 5 |
Please move to first 5 Cars for exit at South Ferry Station

MTA Ⓜ The Transit Authority. Going your way.

SUBWAY CAR POSTER
Circa 1990
Produced by MTA New York City Transit
Recognizing the enormous increase of New York's immigrant population in recent decades—as well as the growth of international tourism to the city—the MTA now posts multilingual notices.

SUBWAY CAR CARDS
1981
Produced by MTA New York City Transit
Bilingual—English and Spanish—posters, using identical layout and designs, became standard for subway safety notices by the early 1980s.

WARNING:
PULLING EMERGENCY BRAKE VALVE STOPS THE TRAIN IMMEDIATELY. IT CAN TAKE UP TO AN HOUR TO RE-START.

 New York City Transit Authority

© 1981 NEW YORK CITY TRANSIT AUTHORITY

IF A PERSON BECOMES SICK, IF YOU SEE SMOKE OR FIRE, IF YOU SEE A CRIME... WAIT UNTIL THE TRAIN IS STOPPED IN THE STATION BEFORE PULLING CORD.

AVISO:
TIRAR EL FRENO DE EMERGENCIA A VALVULA HACE PARAR EL TREN INMEDIATAMENTE. PUEDE TOMAR HASTA UNA HORA PARA VOLVER A PARTIR.

New York City Transit Authority

© 1981 NEW YORK CITY TRANSIT AUTHORITY

SI ALGUIEN SE ENFERMARA, SI USTED VIERA HUMO O FUEGO, SI USTED VIERA UN CRIMEN... ESPERE HASTA QUE EL TREN SE PARE EN LA ESTACION ANTES DE TIRAR EL CORDON.

ROLLING STOCK: CAR DESIGN

Impressive as all the subway stations may be—not to mention the tracks, power plants, train yards, tunnels, and trestles—they amount to very little without the system's moving parts: the subway cars. Their size, shape, and amenities evolved gradually, through dozens of models ordered originally for three separate systems. The most important milestones in their com-

plicated history involve technical advances, but there is also a design story, which runs from a modified version of a late Victorian wooden railroad coach, to an early twenty-first-century computerized, stainless-steel-and-fiberglass subway car.

The first cars to pull up at Heins & LaFarge's drawing-room-style platforms had handsome wood-

MODEL, BMT "AB STANDARD" SUBWAY CAR

Circa 1960

Maker unknown

The sixty-seven-foot-long, ten-foot-wide, all-steel "Standard" served as the workhorse of the Brooklyn Rapid Transit's original subway fleet. Between 1914 and 1924, the BRT and its successor, the BMT, ordered 950 of them. Longer and wider than IRT cars, the Standard had a solid, somewhat blocky look, broken up by its many window and door openings—three sets of double doors per side—and softened by the curves of the roof, clerestory, door openings and windows, and by the then-novel side roll-sign housings. The Standards remained in service until 1969.

and-copper exteriors painted in "Tuscan red" with "burnt orange" trim—journalists called them "flaming burnished sides." Dubbed "composites" because their structure combined wood with steel, they represented an unhappy compromise for their designer, consulting engineer George Gibbs, who had envisioned a fleet of all-steel cars, the world's first. Almost immediately, however, Gibbs found a way to introduce all-steel cars into the subway, and soon these "Gibbs cars" became standard.

Unlike today's cars, the original fifty-one-foot-long models—both composite and all-steel—had entrances only at their ends, through vestibules with sliding doors operated by attendants. Inside, admiring passengers enjoyed mahogany paneling, maple flooring, and handrails with brass fittings, from which hung thirty-eight leather straps that turned

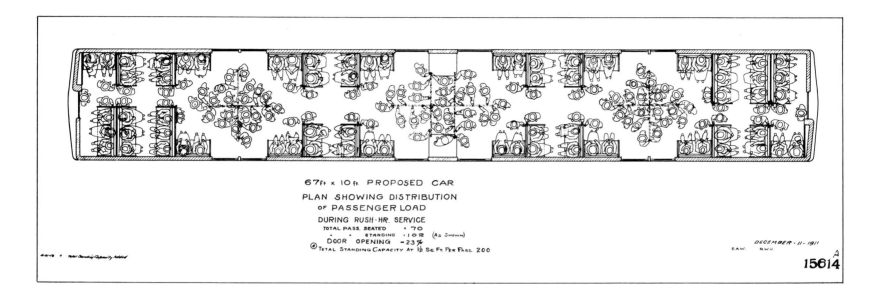

67ft x 10ft PROPOSED CAR
PLAN SHOWING DISTRIBUTION
OF PASSENGER LOAD
DURING RUSH·HR. SERVICE
TOTAL PASS. SEATED · 70
"   " STANDING ·102 (AS SHOWN)
④ DOOR OPENING ·23%
TOTAL STANDING CAPACITY AT 1½ SQ.FT. PER PASS. 200

DECEMBER·11·1911
E.A.W.   R.W.J.

15614

New York City subway riders into "straphangers." Rattan-upholstered seating ran lengthwise along the sides, with crosswise seats in the center of the car. The IRT proudly announced that "all hardware is of bronze, of best quality and heavy pattern, including locks, pulls, handles, sash fittings, window guards, railing brackets and sockets, bell cord thimbles, chafing strips, hinges, and all other trimmings." The overall effect suggested a stripped-down, but still dignified, railroad coach. Over the years, the Gibbs car design underwent various changes—center doors, brass window sashes, improved lighting—but in general, IRT cars maintained the same overall design and all-lengthwise seating configuration until 1940, when the IRT merged into the unified system.

When the BRT started service in 1915, rather than use an IRT-style car (and pay royalties for the privilege) the company introduced its

"Proposed BRT Subway Car Passenger Load During Rush-Hour Service"
December 11, 1911; revised April 21, 1913
Signed "E.A.W." and "R.W.J."
This unusually dramatic overhead view illustrates passenger capacity for the new, all-steel subway cars known as "AB Standards" that went into service in 1915.

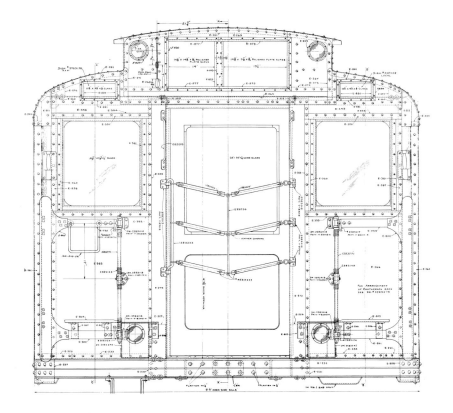

DRAWING, IND R-1 CAR FRONT ELEVATION
Circa 1930
Engineering Department, Board of Transportation of the City of New York

IND R-1 CAR NO. 100
Circa 1930
Manufactured by American Car and Foundry, Berwick, Pennsylvania

own all-steel car, the "Standard." Wider and longer than the IRT cars, the Standard's design acknowledged the first fruits of the subway's great success: constant overcrowding. Based on careful study of railroad cars in other cities, the roomier Standard accommodated more passengers, used a mix of crosswise and lengthwise rattan seating, and significantly eased the strain of crowds entering and exiting the cars by abandoning manually operated vestibule entrances at either end in favor of three double-door pneumatic entrances along the sides. Larger windows, new destination roll-down signs, and, later, brighter lighting all helped create a more modern and efficient look. Instead of Tuscan red, the Standards were painted dark brown and had black roofs.

In 1932, the Independent line introduced the R-1 ("Revenue Contract 1") car. The R-1 combined the roominess of the BMT with the speed of the IRT, but its riveted steel exterior, painted an institutional green, gave it an industrial look suggesting the Depression economics of the day. By contrast, during the same decade, the BMT introduced a series of experimental lightweight, streamlined, multi-section models, including the stainless steel "Zephyr," with red leather upholstery and incandescent lighting, and the aluminum alloy "Blue Bird," with mohair seats and mirrored walls.

Following World War II, the newly unified system embarked on a series of "R" cars that gradually completed the transformation to today's stainless steel and fiberglass models. As early as 1949, the R-11 prototype suggested the look of subways yet to come. Its stainless steel exterior with corrugated sides, its porthole windows and fluorescent lights, all expressed a brave new technology—including

NEW BMT / IND R-11 STAINLESS-STEEL SUBWAY CAR
Promotional Rendering, Circa 1949
Manufactured by Budd Car Company, Philadelphia, Pennsylvania

IND / BMT R-11 PROTOTYPE / R-34 CAR NUMBER 8013
1949
Manufactured by Budd Company, Philadelphia, Pennsylvania
Rebuilt by New York City Transit Authority, 1964–1965
A ribbed stainless-steel body and porthole windows gave
the R-11 a self-consciously modern look, dramatically different
from all earlier subway cars.

an air filtration system with electrostatic dust filters and ultraviolet lamps to kill germs. The *New York Times* dubbed the R-11 "the car of tomorrow." Unfortunately, the R-11 was meant to run on the Second Avenue line, and that particular tomorrow has yet to dawn. The R-11's porthole windows survived in the R-15 of 1950, but not the sleek silvery look—the new car was painted maroon with beige stripes. Stainless steel didn't return until the 1960s, most notably with the R-40, the first cars with successful air-conditioning, introduced with great fanfare into Mayor John Lindsay's "Fun City." Styled by industrial designer Raymond Loewy, the R-40's futuristic exterior included a slanted front end—as though plowing through subway-tunnel winds on a high-speed train.

Until just a few years ago, passengers could sample a variety of subway car models—some old, some new, some repainted, some rebuilt—all operating on the various lines at any given moment. Today's fleet, however, is well on its way to complete standardization. The latest cars grew out of an early 1990s series of experimental "New Technology Test Trains" designed by none other than Massimo Vignelli, under the direction of the MTA's Arts for Transit program, in a process that for the first time incorporated extensive public input. With their spotless stainless steel exteriors and impeccably clean and well-lit, blue and beige, steel and fiber-glass interiors—with ergonomically correct seating and grab bars, and dark, seamless flooring—the new R-142 and R-143 cars have racked up rave reviews and design awards, and transformed the subway experience. Their shiny, utilitarian look and feel match the aesthetic of the MetroCard turnstiles that provide access to them, and, indeed, they owe their design to the same firm, Antenna Design, that created the new MetroCard Vending Machines—bringing a uniform aesthetic to the entire system. New Yorkers are still a little suspicious of the cars' articulate, automated announcements—can this really be the subway?—but the car of tomorrow has apparently arrived and as we enter the subway's second century, passengers are starting to like it.

BMT MULTISECTION CAR, OR "GREEN HORNET"
At Coney Island Yard
Circa 1935
Manufactured by Pullman Car and Manufacturing Corporation, Chicago, Illinois
The Pullman company built just one five-section car for the BMT. Its flared shape and unusual color—aluminum with two shades of green—inspired its widely used nickname, taken from a popular radio and comic book character.

BMT "GREEN HORNET" MULTISECTION CAR INTERIOR
Circa 1935
Manufactured by Pullman Car and Manufacturing Corporation, Chicago, Illinois
Inside the Green Hornet, green gave way to blue for the walls—dark blue below, light blue above, "to provide a colorful, but restful finish"—brown for the leather seat cushions, and a cream tint for the ceiling, all contrasting with stainless-steel window frames and polished aluminum handrails and stanchions.

BMT BLUEBIRD OR COMPARTMENT CAR NO. 8000

At Eighth Avenue, Sea Beach Line, Brooklyn
Circa 1939
*Manufactured by Clark Equipment Company, Battle
Creek, Michigan*

With dark blue and ivory sides, aluminum moldings,
Chinese-red stripes, a deep blue roof, and pale
blue interiors—adorned with mirrored end panels,
bulls-eye lighting, and mohair-covered seats—this
experimental lightweight, three-section unit became
known as a "Bluebird." The Clark company built
the Bluebird with rubber springs and resilient
wheels for "quiet, comfort, safety, [and] speed." The
new cars also incorporated technical and design
elements originally developed for the BMT's
streamlined "Modern Street Car," or PCC Car, with
components built to PCC specifications. Though
advertised as "The Streamlined Car for Subway and
'L' Lines" and the "Compartment Car of Tomorrow,"
tomorrow never came for the Bluebirds—after
creating the prototype in 1938, Clark built only five
additional cars in 1940.

DETAIL, IRT R-12 CAR NUMBER 5760
1948
Manufactured by American Car and Foundry Company, Berwick, Pennsylvania

DETAIL, VELON SEAT COVERING
IRT R-12 Car Number 5760
1948
Manufactured by American Car and Foundry Company, Berwick, Pennsylvania

INTERIOR, IRT R-12 CAR NUMBER 5760
1948
Manufactured by American Car and Foundry Company, Berwick, Pennsylvania
As the first new IRT car ordered in the post-World War II era, the R-12 represented a major break with earlier technology and design. New interior features included enclosed bracket ceiling fans, fluorescent lighting, bar handholds, and synthetic (Velon or Sarran) seat coverings in the green chain and cream background pattern.

IRT R-17 CAR NUMBER 6609

1955

Manufactured by St. Louis Car Company,
St. Louis, Missouri

DETAIL, INDICATOR LIGHTS

BMT Q-Car No. 1612c

Circa 1939

Manufactured by Jewett Car Company, Newark, Ohio
The BMT rebuilt ninety original wooden, open-platform
elevated cars for elevated subway operation to the 1939
World's Fair in Flushing Meadows Park. Improvements
included side lights indicating express or local service.

DETAIL, NEW YORK CITY TRANSIT AUTHORITY LOGO

R-33S Subway Car No. 9306

Circa 1964

The new subway cars acquired for service to the
1964–1965 New York World's Fair Flushing
Meadows Park sported a unique powder-blue-
and-white paint scheme and the new red-and-
blue Transit Authority logo, introduced in 1963.

DETAIL, RATTAN SEAT BACKS
BMT D-Type Triplex Car Number 6095C
1927
Manufactured by Pressed Steel Car Company,
Pittsburgh, Pennsylvania
From 1904 through the end of World War II, passengers enjoyed seat covers made of rattan—a tropical reed, its dried, split stems woven into a fabric backed with canvas. Adapted from earlier streetcars and elevated railway coaches, rattan survived in older subway cars well into the 1960s.

INTERIOR, BMT D-TYPE TRIPLEX CAR NUMBER 6095C
1927
Manufactured by Pressed Steel Car Company,
Pittsburgh, Pennsylvania
To meet increasing passenger volume in the 1920s, the BMT introduced a radically different car design, even larger than the Standard. One hundred thirty-six feet long, and built as three hinged sections, each Triplex matched the size and passenger capacity of two BMT Standards. The 121 Triplexes ordered between 1924 and 1928—solid, durable, and the largest and heaviest of all subway cars—remained in passenger service until 1965. Despite differences in length and door configuration, the Triplex interiors shared many features with the Standards—rattan upholstery, combined cross- and lengthwise seating, porcelain enamel poles and hand-bars, and exposed ceiling fans.

INTERIOR, BMT / IND R-30 CAR NUMBER 8506

1961

Manufactured by St. Louis Car Company, St. Louis, Missouri
The R-30—first of the BMT / IND cars to use an IRT-style
all-lengthwise seating configuration—also introduced
coral-colored hard fiberglass polyester seats.

INTERIOR DETAIL, SIDE ROUTE AND DESTINATION SIGN

BMT / IND R-30 Car Number 8506

Circa 1985

Car Manufactured by St. Louis Car Company, St. Louis, Missouri, 1961
Replacement plastic sign curtains from the 1980s—using
Unimark's Helvetica typeface—contrast with the car's
original housing, dating from 1961.

IRT SUBWAY CAR SIDE ROUTE ROLL SIGN

"3 / 7 Av Express"

Circa 1983

These roll signs, designed according to the revised 1970s
graphics standards, were used on R-21, R-22, R-26, R-29,
and R-36 cars, replacing earlier signs.

RENDERING, PROPOSAL FOR INTERIOR OF R-143
1998
Designed by Antenna Design New York, Inc.

MODEL, R-142 SUBWAY TRAIN
Cars 6301 to 6305
1999
Manufactured by Gad Shaanan Design Inc., Montreal, Canada for Bombardier
Based on the R-110A "new technology" prototype train unveiled in 1992, the R-142 and R-142A subway car series
began arriving in 1999 for operation on the IRT. The 1,630 new cars—1,030 R-142s from Bombardier and 600
R-142As from Kawasaki—replaced the so-called "Red Birds" from the late 1950s and early 1960s. The Red Birds
have since found an ecologically suitable new use, forming an artificial offshore reef along the Atlantic coast

BMT/IND SUBWAY CAR FRONT DESTINATION ROLL SIGN
"Chambers Street"
Circa 1980
Destinator mechanism made by Electric Service
Manufacturing Company, Chicago, Philadelphia, New York
Illuminated roll signs of this type—using white
Helvetica type in both upper- and lowercases on a
black background—were replacements for earlier roll
signs on R-10, R-16, R-27, R-30, R-32, and R-38 cars.

BMT/IND SUBWAY CAR SIDE SIGN BOX WITH ROUTE SIGN
Circa 1985

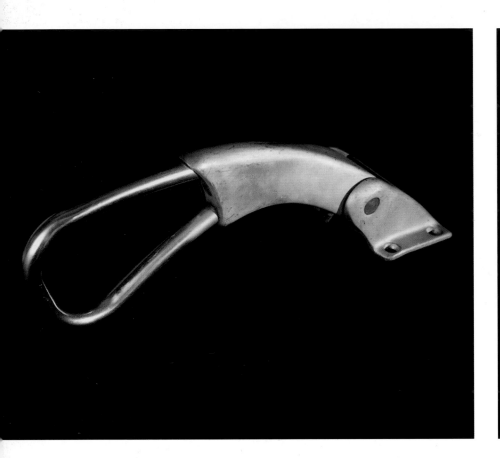

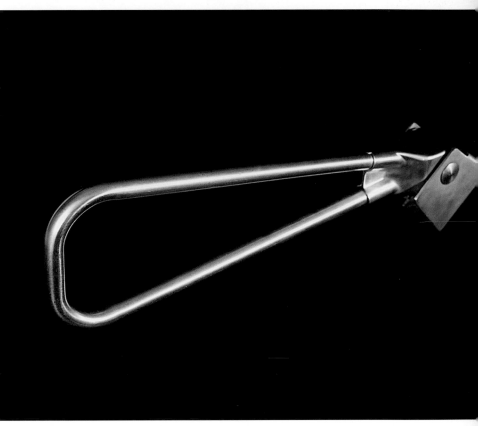

SUBWAY CAR HANDHOLD

Circa 1955

Curved stainless-steel handholds, introduced in subway cars in the mid-1950s, offered a modern version of the porcelain-enamel grab-handles of the 1910s and the leather straps not just of the original IRT subway cars, but also of their nineteenth-century predecessors—trolleys, horsecars, and omnibuses. This model was installed on IND / BMT R-16 cars and IRT R-17s.

SUBWAY CAR HANDHOLD

Circa 1960–1970

Elongated, stirrup-shaped, stainless-steel handholds replaced metal hand-bars in new subway cars during the late 1950s and the 1960s. Hand-bars returned in the R-44s.

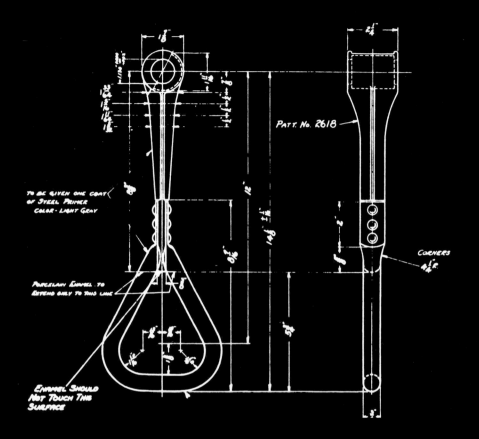

DRAWING
"Type 'E' Loop" Subway Handhold or Grip
Circa 1930

GRAB-HANDLE ASSEMBLY
From IRT "Low V" Subway Car
Circa 1916
Made by Rico Sanitary Straps
Movable, porcelain-handled steel grab-handles for standing
passengers, introduced in IRT subway cars around 1910, offered a
major advance in durability and sanitation over the traditional leather
straps. The IRT operated "Low V" cars from 1916 to 1964.

AFTERWORD

PETER S. KALIKOW, Chairman, Metropolitan Transportation Authority

The extraordinary achievements chronicled and illustrated in this book represent the work of countless designers, artists, architects, engineers, and craftspeople. They also represent a century-long commitment to making New York's subway not just the efficient and dependable transit system we all rely on, but also an attractive environment of which we can all be proud. And they point the way to the system's future, as we build the subway of the twenty-first century.

Over the past decade, we have devoted significant resources to recognizing and restoring the subway's remarkable and unexpected legacy of art and architecture, much of it hidden from view for far too long. At the same time, we have committed ourselves to encouraging excellence in new work through the Arts for Transit program while documenting our achievements for posterity through the New York Transit Museum. Our New Station Planning and Design Guidelines focus on the essentials of safety, security and accessibility, but they also appreciate and encourage fine design. The technologies available to us today would stagger the creators of the original IRT, who, remember, built the subway system largely by hand. Yet we find ourselves working on many of the same issues—materials, finishes, lighting, acoustics, furniture, advertising, and signage.

In 1904, the people who planned the IRT understood it to be a great public work, and in 2004 we feel just the same way. We have exciting projects in the works, from a new, state-of-the-art Fulton Street transit center to completion of the long-awaited Second Avenue line. As we go forward into the new century, we can take our cue from Chief Engineer Parsons, and continue his tradition of building a subway that combines beauty and utility.

ACKNOWLEDGMENTS

GABRIELLE SHUBERT, Director, New York Transit Museum

A project of this magnitude requires the input and insight of a wide variety of skilled and talented individuals. We were lucky at the New York Transit Museum to have assembled a team that brought different perspectives on the subway, and different levels of familiarity with the subway's intricacies. Their lively points of view added up to a compelling whole.

As overall project manager, Transit Museum Curator Carissa Amash showed extraordinary wit, stamina, and dogged commitment to the *Subway Style* exhibit and book. She logged an inordinate number of hours, bringing her impeccable integrity and considerable organizational and curatorial talents to complete the two projects on time. She has the Museum's deepest gratitude. Project assistant Dana Zullo arrived straight out of Columbia University with a highly developed Puritan work ethic, graciously insinuating her good taste and unerring instincts. Principle writer and text editor Anthony Robins and photographer Andrew Garn gave the book a voice and an eye, bringing it to life with their stylish elegance. Researcher John Kriskiewicz offered an architectural historian's intuition about the subway's most unusual stations, guiding us to the jewels and anomalies in a constellation of styles and forms.

Other Transit Museum staff members contributed their valued expertise. Senior Curator Charles Sachs and Curator Amy Kurlan-der used their extensive knowledge of our collections to research, write, and edit captions and labels; Registrar Chandra Buie possesses, in the words of the project manager, "the strength of three men" and ably tracked the whereabouts of some 150 objects from storage to conservator to exhibition and back; Technician Todd Ludlam hauled objects, carefully positioning them to attain their most flattering aspect in the photography studio; Archivist Miriam Tierney located historic images from our collections that added an important perspective on the material, while Assistant Director Junnko Tozaki secured grant funding from the New York State Council on the Arts and other sources; Administrative Manager Angela Agard kept all the records straight.

MTA New York City Transit helped us reveal the often unnoticed assets of the NYC Subway system. Assistant Chief Stations Officer Gricelda Cespedes and Supervisor Donna D'Ambrosio provided access to subway stations, cleaning and lighting station ornaments to facilitate photo shoots. Chief Architect Porie Saikia-Eapen and Architects Tom Fackelman and Vijay Sawant, along with Senior Director Andrew Bata and Project Administrator Hollie Wells, provided invaluable information on the design process, and access to models and historical documents. Consulting architects John diDomenico, Sudhir Jambhekar, and John Tarantino (former chief architect at NYC Transit) gave us insight into current design trends and an

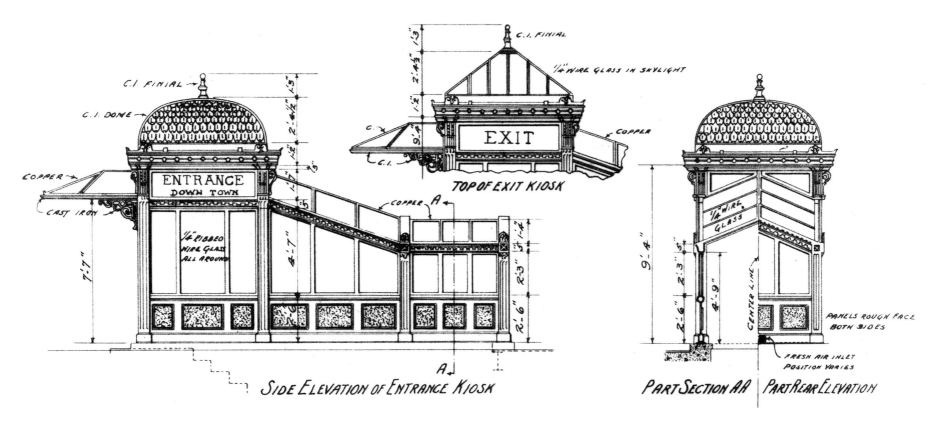

SIDE ELEVATION OF ENTRANCE KIOSK   TOP OF EXIT KIOSK   PART SECTION AA | PART REAR ELEVATION

enlightening comparison with historical practices. Research assistant Michelle Stanek focused on several topics that had eluded us: cartography, advertising, and graphic design; and technical consultant Jonathan Finkelstein brought us an invaluable working tool, the Community Crossings website—allowing all team members to share findings as they emerged.

We are grateful to Noah Lukeman for finding us a publisher. Our editor at Stewart, Tabori & Chang, Marisa Bulzone, has our eternal gratitude for her soothing voice and unruffled manner. Associate Editor Jennifer Eiss and Copyeditor Ana Deboo fine-tuned all the details. Susi Oberhelman created an elegant design that matches the splendor of the subway system itself. Jane Searle ensured that the printing was of equal beauty. And our deepest thanks go to the Metropolitan Transportation Authority for their generous support of the New York Transit Museum, allowing us to preserve the subway's rich history, which in turn plays such a critical role in the history of the city of New York.

SELECTED BIBLIOGRAPHY

Art En Route: MTA Arts For Transit. New York: Metropolitan Transportation Authority, 1994.

Cohen, Paul E., and Robert T. Augustyn. *Manhattan In Maps: 1527–1995*. New York: Rizzoli International Publications, Inc., 1997.

Coppola, Philip Ashforth. *Silver Connections*. Four Oceans Press, 1994.

Cudahy, Brian J. *Under The Sidewalks of New York: The Story of the Greatest Subway System in the World*. New York: Fordham University Press, 1995.

Cunningham, Joseph. *Interborough Fleet*. West Orange, NJ: Xplorer Press, 1997.

Cunningham, Joseph, and Leonard De Hart. *A History of The New York City Subway System: Revised Edition*. USA, 1993.

Fischler, Stan. *The Subway: A Trip Through Time on New York's Rapid Transit*. New York: H&M Productions II Inc., 1997.

Fischler, Stan. *Uptown Downtown: A Trip Through Time on New York's Subways*. New York: Hawthorn/Dutton, 1976.

Framberger, David J., "Architectural Designs for New York's First Subway." *Historic American Engineering Record: Interborough Rapid Transit Subway*. New York: New York City Transit Authority, 1978.

Greller, James Clifford. *New York City Subway Cars*. Belleville, NJ: Xplorer Press, 1995.

Greller, James Clifford. *Subway Cars of the BMT*. Belleville, NJ: Xplorer Press, 1996.

Hood, Clifton. *722 Miles: The Building of the Subways and How They Transformed New York*. Baltimore, MD: Johns Hopkins University Press, 1995.

Interborough Rapid Transit Company. *The New York Subway Its Construction and Equipment*. New York: Interborough Rapid Transit Company, 1904. (Rprt: New York: Fordham University Press, 1991).

Meggs, Philip B. *A History of Graphic Design*. 3rd ed. New York: John Wiley & Sons, Inc., 1998.

Meikle, Jefrey I. *Twentieth Century Limited: Industrial Design in America, 1925–1939*. Philadelphia: Temple University Press, 1979.

Michael Hertz Associates. "Brief Historical Perspective of Recent MTA Subway Maps for a Redesign Program." New York, 1997.

Paintings by Squire Vickers 1872–1947: Designing Architect of the New York Subway System. New York: Shepherd Gallery, Associates, Inc., 1992.

Salomon, George. *Out Of The Labyrinth: A Plea and A Plan for Improved Passenger Information on the New York Subways. Circa 1957*. Salomon Collection, New York Transit Museum Archives.

Sansone, Gene. *Evolution of New York City Subways: An Illustrated History of New York City's Transit Cars 1867–1997*. New York: The New York Transit Museum Press, 1997.

Stern, Robert A.M., Gregory F. Gilmartin, and John M. Massengale. *New York, 1900: Metropolitan Architecture & Urbanism, 1890–1915*. New York: St. Martin's Press, 1995, c1983.

Stern, Robert A.M., Gregory Gilmartin, and Thomas Mellins. *New York 1930: Architecture and Urbanism Between the Two World Wars*. New York: St. Martin's Press, 1994, c1987.

Stern, Robert A.M., Gregory Gilmartin, and Thomas Mellins. *New York 1960: Architecture and Urbanism Between the Second World War and The Bicentennial.* The Monacelli Press, 1995.

Stookey, Lee. *Subway Ceramics: A History and Iconography.* 2nd ed. Vermont: Lee Stookey, 1992.

Tunick, Susan. *Ceramic Ornament in the New York Subway System.* New York: D. Grosser and Associates, c1994.

Unimark International, New York (designers). *New York City Transit Authority Graphics Standard Manual.* New York, 1970.

Vickers, Squire J. "Architectural Treatment of Stations on the Dual System of Rapid Transit in New York City." *Architectural Record.* V.XLV No.1 pp 15 ff, January 1919.

Vickers, Squire J. "Designing Architect." *Public Service Record.* Vol III No.1. January, 1916.

Vickers, Squire J. "The Design and Finish of the Subway Station." and "Discussion." *The Municipal Engineers Journal.* V.19 first quarterly issue, 1933.

Vickers, Squire J. "Design of Subway and Elevated Stations." *The Municipal Engineers Journal.* Vol.3 No. 9 paper 114. November, 1917.

Vignelli, Masssimo and Michael Bierut. *Design:Vignelli.* New York: Rizzoli, 1981.

White, John H., Jr. *The American Railroad Passenger Car.* (2 vols.) Baltimore, MD: Johns Hopkins University Press, 1978.

Wilson, Richard Guy, Dianne H. Pilgrim, Dickran Tashjian. *The Machine Age in America 1918–1941* New York: The Brooklyn Museum in association with Harry N. Abrams, Inc., 1986.

INDEX

Senior Editor: Marisa Bulzone

Principal Writer and Text Editor: Anthony Robins

Associate Editor: Jennifer Eiss

Graphic Production by Jane Searle

Designed by Susi Oberhelman

The text of this book was composed in the Scala Family, designed by Martin Majoor in 1990.

Printed by Toppan Printing Co.

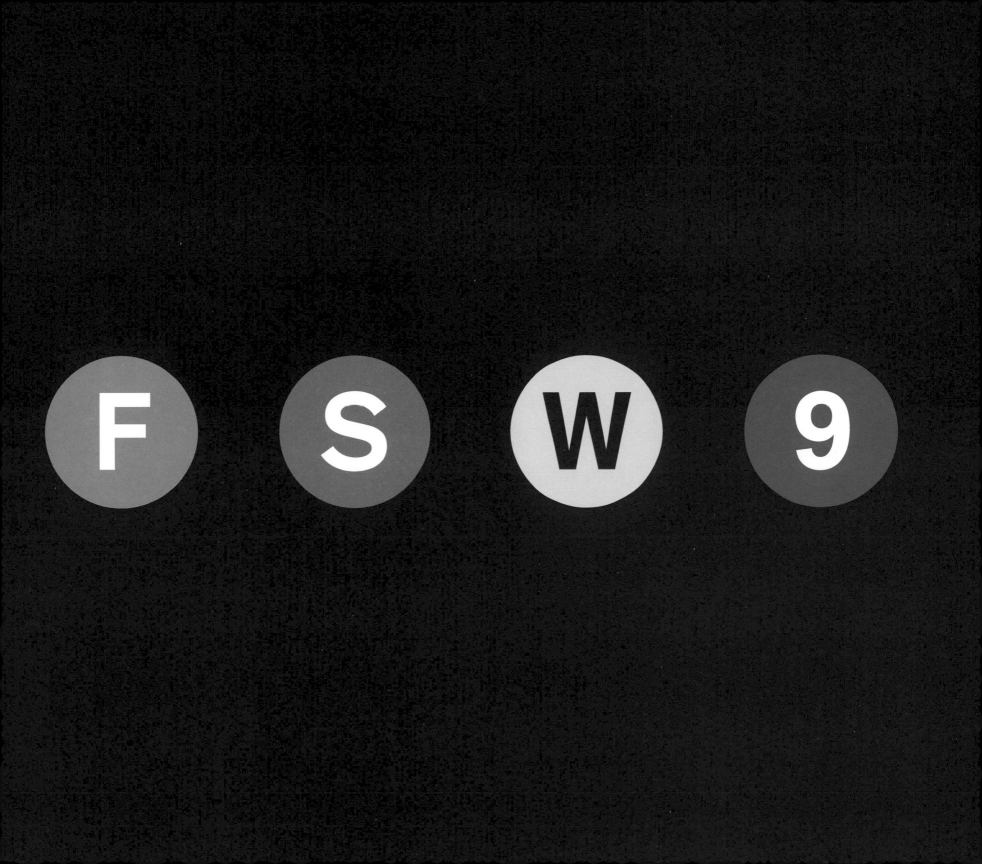